If You Really Knew Me

If You Really Knew Me

A MEMOIR OF MISCARRIAGE and MOTHERHOOD

Mary Purdie

For mothers whose children we cannot see.

table of contents

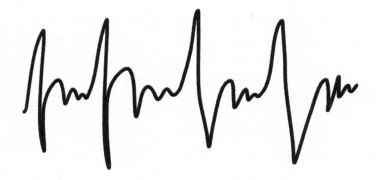

heartbeats

I sat at the edge of the exam table as the doctor wheeled the ultrasound machine closer and turned the monitor toward me. DeAndre was standing at my side, crammed in the corner of the narrow exam room. I placed my heels in the cold plastic stirrups and smoothed the thin white paper sheet over my thighs as I reclined back.

"DeAndre, would you mind turning off the light?" the doctor asked. He flicked the switch on the wall behind him and the ultrasound monitor glowed brighter.

I held my breath as the doctor inserted the ultrasound wand between my legs and moved it around slowly, her eyes fixed on the screen. Laminated posters of illustrated reproductive organs and medical diagrams hung on the pale blue walls of the dim room, their colorful details fading into the blurred background as I stared at the monitor, anxiously listening for a sound—the pitter-patter of a heartbeat that pounded in harmony with my own.

The doctor pointed to a smattering of pixels on the screen. I squinted, trying to make out the image, but it was barely visible on the monitor, which looked like it was built in the 80s and so worn that I wondered why they hadn't retired it. She clicked around on her keyboard, dragging a line across the screen to measure the gestational sac and the peanut inside of it—our baby. A tiny white speck inside the peanut flashed, brightening and dimming in a steady rhythm.

"There's the heartbeat," she said. She paused, observing the movement on the screen. "Hmm. It appears to be slow."

"What does that mean?" I asked.

"I'm afraid it might not be a viable pregnancy," she said. She leaned in closer to the screen.

"How strong is the heartbeat exactly? Can you measure it?"

She turned away from the monitor and removed the probe, then rolled off the clear plastic covering. "I'm not able to get a measurement on it, but it's slower than I'd like," she said. She hooked the ultrasound wand in place next to the monitor and handed me a printout of the sonogram as I sat up. "Let's be cautiously optimistic for now. Six weeks is still very early. We'll have you come back for another ultrasound next week." She took off her gloves, dropped them in the garbage can, and left the room.

I took a deep breath and carefully swung my legs around the side of the exam table. DeAndre handed me my clothes—half-folded jeans with my underwear strategically hidden inside the fabric. I slid them on quickly, buttoning my jeans with shaky hands. I bit down on my bottom lip as I tucked the sonogram printout in my purse.

DeAndre put his hand on the door handle and turned to me. "You good?"

I tilted my head back and raised my eyes toward the ceiling as I blinked back tears. I puffed my cheeks and exhaled all the air from my lungs, straightened my shoulders, and nodded toward the door.

He opened the door slowly, grazing his fingers against the small of my back as I stepped past him and quietly stormed down the hall. We passed by a large collage of glossy photographs, their sharp corners hanging over the edge of the cork board on all sides. I scanned the sea of tightly swaddled newborn babies and rosy infant cheeks staring back at me before shifting my gaze toward the exit. I led us through the waiting area and out into the Los Angeles summer heat.

The doctor's words rang in my ears, the commotion so shrill it drowned out honking car horns and blaring music traveling out of car windows as we walked along Wilshire Boulevard to our car. I got into the passenger seat and slammed the door shut. The inside of the car was an oven, the heat creating wavy shadows that danced across the dashboard. DeAndre slid into the driver's seat and turned to face me. I held the sonogram image to my face with both hands and studied the dark pixels closely. My bottom lip trembled as hot tears trickled down my cheeks.

"What the fuck is this?" I asked, waving the printout. "I can barely see anything on this. Why did she even bother giving this to us?" I dropped the thin, shiny printout in my lap and lowered my face into the palms of my hands. Tears cascaded down, seeping through the cracks between my fingers. DeAndre rested his hand on my shoulder.

"I'm sorry, babe," he said. He rubbed my shoulder lightly. "Look, you're pregnant, and there's a heartbeat. That's all good news, right?"

I quickly turned my head to look at him. "You're not worried?" I asked, accusingly.

"No, I'm not. I really think it's going to be okay," he said.

In our six years together, I'd learned that DeAndre is an excellent hype man, which works out well for me since

I regularly fall into anxious spirals and self-deprecation traps, and often need a hand climbing out. When I find myself neck-deep in negativity, I can tap DeAndre on the shoulder and say, "Hey, I'm struggling. Can you give me a boost, please?" And he gives me his full attention before tossing a bucket of confetti at my wounded ego. "You killed that project, babe! Do you even understand how talented you are? Look at how far you've come! Who cares what anyone thinks? You're on fire! Everything is going to work out, I promise." It is a truly remarkable gift. Sometimes, though, like when I have just been sucker-punched by the reality that the beating heart inside my womb will likely cease at any moment, unwavering optimism is not a trait that I am able to receive gracefully.

I vacantly nodded at DeAndre's effort to catch me as I stumbled toward doom, though I ached for him to swim in this dread with me, to hold my hand and scream together in a chorus of rage.

*　*　*

At home, I stared at the sonogram image some more. I brushed my fingertip over the tiny peanut shape and whispered, "Please make it." I set the picture down next to me on the couch and opened my laptop. I typed into the search bar "slow heartbeat at six weeks." Among the results were a handful of stories across various message boards and blogs. I sifted through them and opened a new tab in my browser for every story with a positive outcome—my favorites were from women who were told their baby had a slow heartbeat, but then it picked up a week later because "the heart probably just started beating that week!" This made sense, so I embraced it as my own narrative, and I imagined myself logging into those same message boards in a week and typing, "Our baby had a slow heartbeat, but it's perfect now. Don't lose hope!"

Between bouts of reading other people's uplifting stories, like taking a drug I was now dependent on, I repeated affirmations. As soon as I blinked my eyes open in the morning, I said out loud, "I am pregnant," and "everything is perfect." I walked around our apartment all day mumbling these affirmations to myself. Every time I went to the bathroom, I stared at my reflection in the mirror while I washed my hands. I held eye contact with myself and affirmed out loud, "I am pregnant. Everything is perfect."

My attempt to force-feed myself positivity was working. I allowed myself to become so deeply hypnotized by false promises that I was no longer grounded in reality. *Good times!* Somewhere inside myself, buried underneath the auto-pilot affirmations and stories from internet strangers, I was aware of the lie I was telling myself—the circus act I was performing to delay being crushed by the familiar weight of loss. I was utterly dependent on this act, though, tossing back toxic positivity like shots of tequila, anything to keep the high going.

* * *

At our next appointment, the doctor brought us into a large exam room with more modern-looking equipment, an upgrade from the vintage piece of crap she'd used at our last ultrasound. I sighed with relief, convinced that the shiny new equipment might be powerful enough to breathe life into my womb. I hiked my fuchsia maxi dress up to my hips and sat on the exam table. I lay back and mentally repeated my affirmations as the doctor began the ultrasound.

The projection on the large flatscreen monitor was bright, and I could spot the fetus right away—it looked like a plump kidney bean. The doctor explained that the baby was measuring five days further than it had measured a week ago. My body tensed as I watched and waited, praying to hear the sweet, rhythmic sound of a tiny, beating heart.

"I'm sorry, there's no heartbeat. It's not a viable pregnancy," she said. She delivered the news so casually. I wondered if she wanted to say, *I told you so.*

"Oh. Okay," I said. The tension in my jaw and shoulders softened, and my body became heavy on the exam table.

Sorrow swung into my heart like a wrecking ball. My posture wilted as I put my feet on the floor and rose from my seat. I reminded myself to breathe. I stood up slowly and let my dress fall over my knees. I slid on my underwear, then my sandals. DeAndre handed me my purse, and we walked swiftly out of the office.

I sank into the passenger seat of our car. DeAndre reached over and lightly squeezed my knee before curling his fingers around mine as he drove us home. Tears trickled from my eyes, the droplets leaving dark spots on the front of my dress.

I stared out the window at palm trees against cloudless blue skies. Our dream of moving out of New York City and planting roots in California was one we'd discussed for five years. I'd envisioned us settling into our Los Angeles apartment as my pregnant belly grew big and round. We'd spend Saturdays preparing the nursery—I'd fold colorful onesies and pastel baby blankets while DeAndre put together the crib. We'd dream out loud about all the memories and traditions we looked forward to creating in the next chapter of our lives.

Our children would grow up on sunshine and beach days, molding wet sand into miniature castles and running away from crashing waves, their high-pitched laughter rippling down the shoreline. Disneyland would be a short drive away, their childhood filled with memories of watching the Electrical Parade on Main

Street seated atop DeAndre's shoulders, fingers sticky with sugar from warm churros.

Moving to California was the easy part. When I found out I was pregnant in February, I applied my meticulous—and admittedly, aggressive—planning tendencies to create spreadsheets, budgets, and set hard deadlines. Our first pregnancy was the catalyst for our cross-country move. I was supposed to arrive in California that summer with a baby kicking in my womb.

Ever since our first ultrasound in February, I'd been reaching for a rush comparable to what I experienced that day—the euphoria that accompanies an audible sign of life growing inside me. I longed to relive that moment, DeAndre standing beside me, my fingers wrapped around his. The sonographer hadn't even prepared us—she clicked a few keys, and we were knocked down by a gentle but mighty thumping sound marching through our eardrums. My eyes filled with tears, and I let the pools grow until they overflowed and dripped down the sides of my face onto the paper sheet beneath my head. DeAndre squeezed my hand lightly, and we exchanged glances, in awe and in love with what we'd created together.

I broke away from my body when the sonographer delivered the sad news with tears in her eyes two weeks later, saying the words I wished I'd never hear uttered in my presence.

"I'm sorry, I can't find a heartbeat."

I believed I would die if I stayed fully present to feel the magnitude of that moment. I thought with absolute certainty, *I cannot make it to the other side of this. I am not this strong.* A few hours later, I had a dilation and curettage, or D&C, a procedure to remove the fetal tissue from my womb, bringing an official end to my beloved but brief pregnancy.

My doctors assured me that it is very common for women to miscarry once and then go on to have full-term pregnancies and healthy babies. Even with their enthusiastic delivery of this vague statistic, it brought me little comfort. I arrogantly believed I deserved to be pregnant more than most.

I had put in grueling work to get to those two pink lines, that first positive pregnancy test. I read the books and bought the ovulation strips. I took my temperature every morning in the 5 a.m. darkness before squatting in the bathroom to poke my cervix. I plugged all this information into a fertility app on my phone, which created a chart to study my cycles in depth. I sipped herbal teas that promised to strengthen my pelvic floor and thicken my uterine lining. I lay under a thermal blanket for 30 minutes each week with acupuncture needles sticking out of my body to boost my chances of an embryo implanting. With equal parts desperation and determination, I white-knuckled my way to conception. And then, the rug was pulled out from under me.

By April, I'd dusted myself off and became immersed in controlling two outcomes: getting pregnant again and moving to California. One thing I knew for sure—we needed to get the fuck out of New York. I had convinced myself that physical distance was the only remedy capable of stitching my broken heart back together. Every corner of our apartment, the streets I walked every day, the subways, the local coffee shop—they were all tainted by memories of being pregnant. I couldn't imagine continuing on like that, the inescapable sadness of those daily reminders peppering every mundane moment.

I didn't have to imagine it, though. I would be living it now as our life in California was off to a somber start. The following week, I made an appointment at a different facility, not by choice, but because our insurance changed on September 1st, two days after we'd learned I was miscarrying for the third time.

* * *

"I've already seen a doctor at another facility, and she confirmed the miscarriage," I said to the nurse. I sat in a chair next to her desk and watched her type notes on her computer as I spoke.

"How far along are you?" she asked.

"I'm supposed to be eight weeks, but it stopped growing before seven weeks," I said. I handed her the sonogram printout, the edges of the paper weathered, corners curled inward. "There was a slow heartbeat here, but then it was gone a week later."

She looked at the printout for a moment. "I'm going to go show this to the doctor. I'll be right back," she said. She disappeared down the hallway.

I leaned my head against the wall behind me and took in a long, deep breath.

The nurse turned the corner into her station two minutes later. "The doctor thinks it might be too early for a heartbeat," she said. She smiled as she handed the sonogram printout back to me and sat down at her desk.

"What? No. I'm telling you... there *was* a heartbeat. We saw it on the ultrasound. And then it stopped."

The nurse nodded. "Follow me," she said.

I poked my head into the waiting room and waved DeAndre over. We followed the nurse into an exam room.

"Undress from the waist down. The doctor will be with you shortly," she said. She handed me a folded paper sheet before leaving the room.

I took off my pants and held up the sheet by two corners, shaking out the folds. I climbed onto the exam table and draped the stiff paper sheet over my legs. A few minutes later, the doctor came into the room, appearing confused as she looked over my chart. I wondered what notes she was reading about me—perhaps a warning: *Patient is agitated, will argue with you.* She looked up from the manila folder and shook my hand, then DeAndre's.

"Nice to meet you both," she said. "I see that your pregnancy test came back positive, but you believe that you're miscarrying. Is that correct?"

"Yes. It's a long story but basically what happened is we lost a pregnancy at eight weeks in March. That was my first pregnancy. I got pregnant again in July, but I miscarried right away. A chemical pregnancy, I think they're called?"

She looked at me like I just told her I'd given birth to an alien. "Huh? A 'chemical pregnancy'?" She enunciated the words slowly as if I'd just invented them on the spot. "I've never heard of that," she said. She stood up and turned her back to me as she washed her hands in the sink.

I wanted to tell her to fucking google it like I did that morning when I woke up bleeding two days after finding out I was pregnant. "Oh, it's a really early miscarriage. I thought that's what they're called. Anyway, I got pregnant four weeks later, and there was a slow heartbeat at six weeks, but now it's gone. So, yeah, I'm having another miscarriage," I said.

"Let's have a look," she said. She rolled the ultrasound machine from the corner of the room and pulled on a pair of blue vinyl gloves. I lay back resigned, knowing that the invasive exam would show no sign of life. I glanced at the screen and noticed that the gestational sac had grown, our baby a speck inside the large black bubble. "Hmm. It doesn't look good, but it could be too early still. Let's have you come back in a week to confirm," she said. She stood up and turned away from me as she peeled off her gloves.

I fought back tears, increasingly aware that an emotional outburst would not be met with compassion here.

"But there *was* a heartbeat," I said. My temper was rising. "I don't want to go home and wait. I know that I've miscarried, and I want to move forward."

The doctor shook her head, holding firm. Despite all the evidence I had laid out, and my deep understanding of what was happening inside my body, they would not allow me to act on my decision to complete my miscarriage until they could see for themselves the following week that there was no fetal heartbeat.

*　*　*

I went home and descended into inconsolable despair, merely trying to stretch the time between swells of tears. I lay in bed sobbing as I dug my fingers into my soft belly, fantasizing about reaching through my flesh so I could rip out my womb, a graveyard rotting inside my body.

Nausea haunted me without mercy, a constant reminder of our seemingly endless misfortune. Morning sickness, fatigue, extreme sensitivity to smells, mood swings—many women I knew complained about these symptoms of pregnancy, but I cherished them, lovingly opening my arms every time a new wretched symptom fell into my lap. *Welcome, miserable friends. Make yourselves at home.* With no evidence to back it up, I'd convinced myself that horrendous symptoms equaled a normal, healthy pregnancy. The worse I felt, the less I'd worry. The joke was on me. There was no longer life growing inside me, but my body carried on as if there was, taunting me as I tended to my broken heart.

I found myself standing in front of the open refrigerator, clinging to normalcy as I looked for something to prepare for lunch. As I scanned the shelves —half-empty with only a package of deli meat, a block of cheese, apples, grapes, a carton of eggs, and a bag of spinach rapidly losing its freshness—the last frayed string that was holding my seams together suddenly snapped.

I let the refrigerator door swing shut, and I collapsed to my knees. I banged my fists into the hard linoleum while tears rained down, a few plump, wet drops landing on the floor in front of me. A stream of harsh words flooded my mind, each one directed at my body. *You broken piece of shit. Why can't you get this right? I hate you!* I squeezed my fists harder, digging my nails deep into the palms of my hands and leaving a row of tiny crescent moon impressions.

I turned to DeAndre, who was sitting at his desk in the dining room with his back to me and his headphones on.

"Why don't fucking you care?!" I screamed, my voice soggy and strained.

DeAndre turned around, lowered his headphones to rest on his shoulders, and stared at me as I came undone like a spinning roll of yarn on the kitchen floor. He appeared unemotional, cloaked in cold, steely armor.

I raised my fists in the air and smashed them into the floor again. My face burned red, my skin bloated and drenched with tears. "WELL?!"

"What do you want me to do, Mary?" he asked. His tone was biting, and as he spoke, the fire in my belly roared.

"Take some of the fucking blame! Did you ever think that maybe this isn't my fault, maybe there's something wrong with *you*?!"

DeAndre turned back around and shook his head as he put his headphones over his ears.

I lay on my side, closed my eyes, and curled my knees toward my chest. Hot air blowing from the bottom of the refrigerator brushed against my bare feet, the soft warmth bringing up memories of being eight-years-old—sitting curled up on our red brick fireplace on a Sunday evening, toasty air wafting through the open weave of the black metal screen, kissing my skin. Across the room, my mom sat on the edge of the couch, folding laundry while *I Love Lucy* reruns played on the TV.

I was seven-years-old when my mom accepted a full-time job in Santa Barbara, a three-hour drive from our home in Orange. Her lengthy commute was impossible to endure daily, so she was only able to be home on the weekends. From the second I stepped in the house and dropped my backpack on the living room floor on Friday afternoon, I eagerly awaited our end of the week ritual—seeing headlights brighten our street through the front window and hearing my mom's white Honda pull into the driveway. Sometimes I'd run outside to greet her, bursting through the screen door as moths fluttered around our porch light and crickets chirped like a choir echoing down the block. The stale loneliness of the past five days dissolved with the late-night sounds of car doors opening and keys rattling.

Some weekends, or longer during our summer break, my mom scooped up me and my big sister Gretchen and drove us to Santa Barbara where we stayed in a guesthouse on her boss's property, complete with a swimming pool that we took advantage of on hot afternoons. In the early evenings, with wet hair and damp bathing suits under our shorts, we'd walk to the corner store for blue and red snow cones or vanilla Drumsticks to satisfy our ravenous post-swimming hunger.

Other weekends, my dad took Gretchen and me on long Saturday morning bike rides around Orange County. We'd ride in a single file line, Gretchen and I wearing matching white helmets decorated with metallic confetti stickers. We'd shout into the wind as we shifted gears, pressing our feet onto our pedals to climb long, steady hills. We always ended up at a cafe some miles away, where we'd shake out our legs and indulge in a breakfast of warm ham and cheese croissants with ice-cold orange juice. When we got back home, we'd tell my mom all about our adventures and show off our battle wounds— mud-splattered legs from surprise puddles, and sweaty hair mashed down from our big, plastic helmets.

I was eight-years-old when I wrote and illustrated *The Lost Puppy*, a book about a puppy named Kathy who runs away from home because she feels neglected and unloved. Kathy finds a friend, Sarah, at the local junkyard, who takes her in and shows her all the love and affection she'd been missing at home. The story ends with Kathy's family showing up at Sarah's house begging Kathy to come home, proving that they had actually loved her all along.

I remember presenting the story to my mom when she came home that weekend. I straightened the pages of *The Lost Puppy* into a neat pile before handing it to her, my hands stained with marker streaks of every color. Years later, she would tell me of reading *The Lost Puppy*, "I was so afraid I'd screwed you up by being away so much." All

I had were warm memories, so it surprised me to hear her confess that the story broke her heart. It wasn't until she shared this with me that I realized I was pouring my heartache onto those pages.

Alone in the living room, my upper body spilled over the walnut-stained wooden coffee table as orange evening light glowed through the window, I put the tip of my fat Mr. Sketch cinnamon-scented marker to white paper and created Kathy, a small brown dog with black spots who wore a pink bow on her head. With my dad fighting heavy Los Angeles traffic on his way home from work, and my older brothers busy with sports or after school jobs, that left Gretchen in the kitchen cooking us dinner —something easy that an 11-year-old could handle like microwavable chicken nuggets or canned baked beans with cut-up hot dogs.

With both knees pressed into our pale gray living room rug as I dragged my markers across paper, I imagine young Mary must have longed to look over and see my mom matching up socks from the clean laundry basket, both of us belly-laughing at Lucille Ball shoving handfuls of chocolate bonbons into her mouth.

I opened my eyes and stared into the shadowy three-inch space under our kitchen cabinets, dust settled into the crevices, a small piece of diced onion that must have fallen, unnoticed, days before. Another wave crashed behind my eyes and I wept until my eyeballs burned, parched and bloodshot.

I wished I would have answered DeAndre's question honestly. *What do you want me to do, Mary?* What I wanted was for him to join me on the floor and hug me so tightly that it forced the air from my lungs. I prayed he would see me in my unbearable misery, falling to pieces like crumbs on the kitchen floor, and rush to my side with the speed of a superhero. I imagined he'd say, "Oh babe, if I could tear your pain away and carry it on my shoulders, I would. I love you so much." I wanted the sound of my voice to smash into him so hard that it cracked his armor, and he'd look at me with his dark brown eyes, and I would know that my screams had a safe home in his presence.

I resented having to explain what I wanted from him, to tell him that I needed him to be close to me and suffocate me with love—so I continued to be mean to him, hoping that the seed of blame I planted would grow into a mountain of guilt. With all my strength, I pushed DeAndre away, going about my day as if he wasn't there. Pushing him away out of spite didn't have the impact I'd hoped for—DeAndre seemed comfortable and relaxed behind the wall he'd built, neither of us anywhere near ready to extend an olive branch to the other.

* * *

We returned to the medical facility to see a different doctor for the follow-up ultrasound. I summarized our situation again, weary from repeating the story. The doctor nodded along as I spoke.

"I wouldn't make any decisions just yet," he said. "It might be best to check again in a few days before moving forward."

I wondered if they'd ever seen a six-week-old fetus die and come back to life. "I've been through this before. I don't need to come back in a few days to confirm. I'd like to go home and induce the miscarriage with medication. *Please.* This is miserable for me," I said, my voice breaking.

"Okay, okay, I understand. Let me see what I can do," he said. He left the room.

DeAndre turned to me and looked me in my eyes for the first time in days. "They're just following procedure. I know this is hard, but it's going to be okay," he said.

I turned my head toward him and furrowed my brows. "You don't know what this feels like—it's not happening inside *your* body!"

His lips parted, but he hesitated to speak right away. "You know what—fine," he mumbled and leaned back in his chair.

The doctor creaked open the door, and I straightened my posture. "Okay," he said. "I'm going to put in the prescription for the medication. You can go to the pharmacy to fill it right away and take the medication tonight if you want."

I exhaled. "Thank you," I said. I began to scoot off the exam table.

"Wait," he said. "I want you to know what to expect. You are going to bleed a lot. Okay?"

I paused, perched on the edge of the padded table. "Yeah. Okay," I nodded.

"I mean, whatever you *think* is a lot of blood, it's going to be *way* more than that," he said. He waited for me to confirm I'd understood before breaking eye contact.

* * *

When we got home, DeAndre and I wandered back into our chosen realities, still worlds apart from one another. He sat at his desk in the dining room. I retreated to the couch. I put the bottle of pills on the coffee table and looked at the time. The doctor had instructed me to get started in the evening so that the worst of the miscarriage would be over by morning and, if I'm lucky, I might be able to sleep through most of it.

At 5 p.m., I sat on the toilet and inserted all four tablets, tucking one on each side of my cervix. I returned to the couch, curled up under a cozy blanket, and waited. Every twinge in my belly gave me pause as I anticipated a clear signal that it was time to run to the toilet.

Around 9 p.m., my lower abdomen started violently cramping, as if someone was wringing out my uterus like a wet washcloth. I slid my hand under the waistband of my pants and rested it on my low belly—my skin was hot. I scooted off the couch and inched toward the bathroom, squeezing my thighs tightly together, remembering the doctor's words about the amount of blood that would soon escape my body.

As soon as I sat on the toilet, what felt like a bucket of blood spilled out of me. When the heavy spill slowed to a light trickle about 20 minutes later, I returned to my corner of the couch and rested, my body curled in a fetal position on my side, until the next wave of heavy cramps thundered in my belly.

I brought my pillow and iPad on my second trip to the bathroom. I leaned the iPad against the wall, opened Netflix, and turned on *The Office*. I sat on the toilet with my torso curled over my pillow for 45 minutes before my heavy eyelids started to droop, and my legs tingled with pins and needles. Around midnight, I put a thick white pad in my underwear and tucked myself into bed next to DeAndre, who was fast asleep in the dark bedroom.

Sunlight illuminated the edges around our blinds as I blinked my eyes open the next morning. I rolled over and rested my hand on the space next to me—it was cool to the touch. DeAndre had been awake for a while. I lay on my back and cradled my low belly in the palms of my hands.

*   *   *

DeAndre drove us to our follow-up appointment two days later, a final ultrasound to confirm that the medicine had done its job. My womb was vacant, yet again.

"What do you suggest we do now?" I asked the doctor.

"You can keep trying," he said, shrugging his shoulders as if I'd asked a ridiculous question.

"Wait, really?" I asked, taken aback. "Don't you think we should figure out why I keep having miscarriages?"

"If you want to see a specialist, you should. But I'm comfortable if you just want to keep trying too," he said.

I looked at DeAndre, but he didn't return my gaze. I turned back to the doctor. "I would like to see a reproductive specialist before we try again. Thank you."

As DeAndre and I walked to our car, I attempted to break the days-long silence by doing what I do best—obsessively planning for the future.

"I'll research specialists and see if we can get an appointment," I said.

DeAndre nodded slowly. I stared at him, trying to read his body language as we got into our car, but he appeared stoic, unmoved. He drove us through the parking garage, down the ramp, and turned onto the street before he finally spoke.

"I think we should wait a few months before we do anything," he said.

My instincts told me to tread lightly. "Um, well, I was thinking we could make an appointment with a specialist to see what's going on," I said. "Just to see. We don't have to do anything with the information right away, but it would be helpful to know so we can plan accordingly. Don't you agree?"

He paused, took a deep breath, and blinked once slowly. I knew what that meant—he was choosing his next words carefully. I glared at him with bated breath.

"I think we need to just relax for a while," he said.

"But... What if there's a major problem?! And then we've wasted precious time by waiting to find out about it!" I argued.

"Well, then, that's just something we'll deal with. Mary, we have been through *too much*. We just... we need to chill," he said. His words hung in the air for a moment before dripping all over my skin like prickly, pouring rain.

I bit my lip and decided not to say another word. Our foundation had been rocked, the pillars beneath us cracked and threatening to buckle, to crumble at the next sudden movement. DeAndre was right—we *had* been through too much. But the idea of waiting, letting time pass while we do nothing to remedy the problem, was completely unnatural to me. From the moment I decided to throw my entire heart into trying to have a baby, my identity was wrapped up in my desire to be a mother. There would be no other path, no change in destination.

dead ends

At home, I didn't know what to do with my time. Normally, I'd spend hours every day scouring miscarriage message boards, taking notes to bring to doctor's appointments, requesting tests that a stranger on the internet told me about. Those rabbit holes where I once found relief were dark and hollow now. I agreed to slow down, to press pause, but this wasn't easy for me. My hands missed the smooth plastic of pregnancy tests from my incessant test-taking, which began every cycle precisely eight days after I ovulated. My self-worth was being peeled away and discarded every day that I didn't open my fertility app, eager to plug in my temperature and note the texture of my cervix. Our whole lives, we are told our bodies are designed to do this. So why couldn't mine? And what was I supposed to do if I couldn't be a mother, the one role I desired above all others?

These questions poured through my mind like heavy rain as I sat at home staring out the window, lying motionless on the couch. I berated myself for not having a life outside of this sole desire, for making the choice one year ago to shrug off any lingering career goals and step into the role I wanted more than anything in the world—to be someone's mom.

When I was a teenager, I envisioned a future where I was a successful and beloved artist. I'd brought all the confidence and praise I'd collected through childhood—from my sophisticated still-life drawings of peanut butter sandwiches and bowls of fruit that I made with my grandma's old oil pastels, and creative projects like The Lost Puppy—into adolescence and young adulthood where I rarely, if ever, questioned my talent. Throughout my youth, family members and teachers affirmed what I believed about myself—that art wasn't just something I was good at, it was the core of my identity.

During the second semester of my senior year of high school, my AP Art teacher, Mrs. Katchen, submitted my portfolio along with two other students' to the prestigious Advanced Placement panel of judges. The judges would select pieces from a large number of portfolios submitted from all over the state of Colorado, where we lived at the time, to be awarded at a special evening ceremony in downtown Denver in the spring. In 2001, I believed this was the highest honor for a high school art student, and my portfolio was selected by Mrs. Katchen as a top contender.

A few weeks later, I learned that my portfolio was the only body of work from my class that was entirely rejected by the panel. Mrs. Katchen quietly shared the news with me one afternoon after the bell rang. I nodded as if it was no big deal, but I was clenching my jaw so hard I was afraid I'd break a tooth. I slid off my stool and haphazardly shoved my sketchbook and pencils into my backpack, racing against my rising tears. Mrs. Katchen was studying me, clearly unconvinced by my display of apathy. When the last remaining students trickled out of the classroom, I relaxed my jaw and sobbed into my hands. I pulled the long sleeves of my cardigan sweater over my hands and wiped my tears with the woven fabric.

Mrs. Katchen, a petite but fierce presence, with brown hair that hung in a low ponytail all the way down her back, thick blunt cut bangs, and colorful dangling earrings, rose to the balls of her feet and wrapped her arms around my shoulders. "Mary, you don't need those people to validate you," she said. She repeated it twice more as she stared into my eyes. Her furious expression made me believe what she really wanted to say was, "Fuck those judges, Mary."

I drove home in tears, stomped up to my bedroom, and cried into my pillow for an hour. That evening, I asked my mom to take a polaroid of me with my eyes closed and my hands pressed over my ears in dramatic fashion, and I used it as reference for my next portrait, illustrating my sadness in shades of white pencil on black Canson paper.

That single rejection at 18-years-old left a lasting wound on my identity. Although I attended Otis—my dream art school—the following year, where I got decent grades and spent four years becoming a better artist and designer, rejection was a sore spot and a trend that continued for years after I graduated college, like a bruise slowly spreading across my skin.

By the time DeAndre and I got engaged, I was working as a corporate receptionist. More than 10 years after graduating from art school, I had little to show for it other than a whole lot of interview experience, a mountain of student loan debt, and a roster of mostly odd jobs: Starbucks barista, production assistant, juice bar cashier, retail salesperson, receptionist.

DeAndre listened to me complain endlessly about my day job—where I did little more than resolve conference room conflicts, smile at unfriendly senior associates, and order office supplies from Staples—and he encouraged me to carve out time to draw, to keep creating, even if it was only a hobby. I'd spend evenings at home sketching characters, brainstorming funny one-liners, and playing with art supplies I hadn't touched in a decade—blendable markers, watercolor and acrylic paints. I spent every weekend working on small art projects, and as I became reacquainted with the only passion I'd ever known in my 30-something years, it grew into an all-consuming love affair.

I signed up for a six-week-long evening course at The New School where I discovered an area of focus that lit my heart up: designing and illustrating greeting cards. After the course ended, I revised my designs based on my classmates' critiques and the professor's feedback, printed them in small batches, and started selling them on Etsy. Around Valentine's Day and Mother's Day, I rented a table for $100 at a local art market in Brooklyn and set up spinning racks and handmade signage to advertise my shop and sell my cards.

My side project was an enormous source of pleasure, but it wasn't a lucrative business. All the money I made from sales went toward printing and supplies, and I barely broke even most months. I decided to submit a few crowd favorite designs to various greeting card companies in an attempt to get some passive income in the form of a licensing deal, but I was either turned down or never received a response. This time, the rejection hardly fazed me. My next big role was coming up, and once we got married and started trying to get pregnant, I shelved my little art business and turned my love of drawing back into a part-time hobby. It wasn't that I didn't believe I could have both a child and a creative career. My decision to stop pursuing art as a living was a deliberate coping mechanism—a declaration that *I* would have the last word in this cycle of rejection.

Now the edges of my identity were bleeding deep purple and crimson, the bruise ripening. Motherhood was rejecting me too. I was speeding toward a dead end, a big red sign telling me WRONG WAY. My head spun until I was dizzy—out of directions, out of ideas. *Who will I be if not a mother? What is my higher purpose if not to birth and nurture another soul?*

* * *

I sat at my desk in our dining room and took out my sketchbook and pencils. I scribbled a list of ideas for miscarriage sympathy cards and spent the next week painting a small number of watercolor cards that expressed sentiments like "I will cry with you" and "Having empty arms makes you no less a mother" and "It's so fucking unfair." I opened a new Etsy shop and listed them, offering to handwrite a message inside on behalf of the buyer, and send it directly to the recipient. I knew from experience that time was of the essence, and this was a way I could pay it forward to another grieving mother.

I perused job sites, aware that I'd need a distraction and an income to carry me to the other side of this prolonged pause or else I'd pull all my hair out from boredom. My criteria was simple: it had to be close to our apartment because I was still stiff with terror every time I had to drive—an outcome of nine years living in New York City where I relied entirely on public transportation—and it had to be part-time. Bonus points if I enjoyed the work and got along well with my co-workers. I needed a job where I could work while pregnant and transition seamlessly into being a stay-at-home mom when our baby was eventually born.

When I saw that a salon around the corner was hiring a receptionist, I perked up my shoulders. I'd walked by The Local Salon a handful of times since we moved into the neighborhood and peeked through the windows at the inviting decor—hand-painted signage, beehive mirrors climbing the wall, exposed brick, and a chic vintage couch in the waiting area. In a bizarre coincidence, the first time I walked by over a month ago, I pulled up their website on my phone to see if they were hiring. I had relevant experience from working at a salon when I lived in New York, one of my many odd jobs, so I knew what it entailed. I wasn't actively looking for work yet, not knowing what traumatic events would lie immediately ahead of me, but the salon's aura was so magnetic, I wanted to be a part of it.

"This is a sign," I said. I submitted my resumé online.

* * *

I met Rosie, the salon's owner, on a Wednesday morning a few weeks later. Rosie had dark merlot-colored hair cut just below her jawline and green eyes that complemented her cherry red lips. Her arms were mostly covered in tattoos and she wore mustard yellow shoes that made me want to invite myself to go shopping with her. She led me up a narrow spiral staircase into a loft space that overlooked the main salon floor. I sat in a velvet soft teal blue chair in the corner behind her station and we chatted about the job for a few minutes before we began bonding over common interests like *Broad City* and our favorite makeup brands. Rosie hired me on the spot, and I started my new job in late September.

I worked at the salon two or three days a week, opening in the mornings, checking guests in and out, rotating towels and robes from the washer to the dryer, and spending a good portion of my paycheck on smoothie bowls and iced almond milk lattes from the neighboring businesses. Even on the most stressful and chaotic days, when every stylist's schedule was booked solid and some clients were rude to me over the phone, I was in the company of kindness surrounded by my new co-workers, confirming that this job was exactly what I'd hoped it would be—a warm and welcome distraction from depressing mornings lying in bed, convincing myself to get up. Going to work was a vacation from the miscarriage message boards, endless internet research, and flipping through channels on the TV only to be repeatedly slapped in the face by another fucking ClearBlue pregnancy test commercial—my miscarriage blues exacerbated every 15 minutes by happy people celebrating a positive pregnancy test.

* * *

Not long after I started working at the salon, I got my first haircut with Alyssa. One of my co-workers lovingly described Alyssa as "kind of a hippie," and the first time I met her, I understood why. Alyssa wore harem pants almost daily, with pretty beaded jewelry and shiny stones that hung from long chains around her neck. She had long blond hair with flawless beach waves, and her smile was as warm as the sun.

Alyssa's station was upstairs on the loft level of the salon. Three large crystals, each one nearly the size of my fist, sat on the shelf along the bottom edge of her mirror. Powder pink, amethyst, and milky stones sparkled in the sunlight that beamed through the windows. The pink stone reminded me of one that a psychic tried to sell me on my fourth date with DeAndre more than six years ago. Walking through the East Village that Saturday night, we saw a sandwich board on the sidewalk up ahead advertising $10 psychic readings. Feeling spontaneous, intoxicated by our budding young love, we stopped to get readings.

My psychic nodded at DeAndre through the window of the storefront and simply said, "He's your soulmate." I blushed, hoping she was right. Before I left, she encouraged me to buy a pretty pink crystal for $60. I politely declined without even listening to her entire pitch.

As I walked through the salon before locking up for the night, I saw Alyssa's crystals lined up on the hardwood floor against the window, little jagged mountains basking in the moonlight. Confused, I did a double-take, but let them be, assuming this was another one of her "hippie" quirks.

"I'm holding a new moon circle at my house next week," Alyssa said one afternoon while we were sitting at reception waiting for her next client to arrive. "You're welcome to come."

"What is that?" I asked.

"It's a small group of women who gather together and we set our intentions for the new moon. I do it every new moon, so if you can't make it, maybe next time," she said.

I had never heard of a new moon circle, and I didn't ask any follow-up questions. I simply responded the same way I had when the East Village psychic tried to sell me a crystal to enhance my love life—politely nodded and then immediately forgot about it.

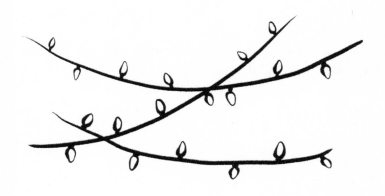

difficult days

Photos highlighting Pregnancy and Infant Loss Awareness Month were sprinkled throughout my social media feeds as we stepped into the first week of October. I scrolled through photos and observed all the ways people coped with October—women and couples lighting candles, writing letters to the children they'd lost, building miniature altars complete with sonogram photos, embroidered quilts, and poems. Fitting, I suppose, that the due date of our first pregnancy landed in the second week of October.

I'd planned to be well into another pregnancy by October 13th, convinced that another baby on the way would distract us, if only a little, from the one we lost before we could blow raspberry kisses on his belly and play *This Little Piggy* while softly tugging his toes. I'd acknowledge the date out loud as I made coffee that morning, and when I'd bring DeAndre his mug, I'd lean down and wrap my arms around his shoulders a few seconds longer than usual. I'd light a candle in the evening and pour my words into an Instagram caption commemorating our loss, but I'd be smiling into the bright light of my phone because, unbeknownst to my internet friends, there was another seed sprouting, a fresh garden growing in my womb.

The weight of dread was a boulder in my belly, growing heavier as the due date drew closer. My arms were empty, and now so was my womb. I struggled with what to do about that single calendar day, a 24-hour burden. I couldn't ignore it if I tried, but I didn't want to do something overly sentimental, either—no need to twist the knife.

"Do you want to go out to dinner on the 13th?" I asked DeAndre.

"Why the 13th?" he asked. He turned around in his desk chair to look at me. Then, a second later, "Oh. Yeah, we can do whatever you want." He turned back around toward his computer.

"Okay. Nothing fancy, just… you know," I said. I stared at the back of his head as he nodded.

* * *

That Thursday evening, I pulled on a pair of black skinny jeans and a sheer burgundy blouse. I pinned my hair up in a topknot and slid my feet into black suede high heels. DeAndre came out of the room in a chambray button-up shirt, dark wash jeans, and a pair of fresh-out-of-the-box sneakers from his ever-growing collection—a tower of Nike boxes stacked in our closet. I glided on two layers of Girl About Town—my longtime favorite shade of magenta lipstick—and looked myself over once in the bathroom mirror before flicking off the light.

DeAndre was standing near the front door, looking at his phone. I leaned into him and put my hand on his low back, my attempt at flirting. He curled his lips into a half-smile, turned, and reached for the door handle.

We walked downstairs to the restaurant, a gastropub across the street from our building. I couldn't remember the last time we'd allowed ourselves an evening out together, a few hours reserved for romantic bliss. We'd clink our drink glasses together and share bites of food as we critiqued every dish, using words we learned from watching *Food Network*. We'd reminisce about funny memories—like the first time DeAndre mixed a drink for me at his apartment in New Jersey and the bottle of club soda exploded all over him. We'd carelessly laugh like we once had before our hearts were fractured by the loss of a child we'd only met in our dreams.

The hostess seated us at a small table in the middle of the half-empty restaurant. A football game was playing on the TV that hung on the wall behind me. DeAndre stared at the TV while I gazed at him for a moment that stretched so long, I wondered if he'd forgotten I was there. I draped my napkin over my lap and opened my menu.

"Should we get an appetizer?" I asked.

DeAndre looked down at his menu. "If you want to." He shrugged his shoulders.

I looked at him and furrowed my brows. I closed my menu and set it on the table without breaking eye contact, though it wasn't returned—he put his menu down and shifted his gaze back to the football game.

The waitress brought our drinks—red wine for me, gin and tonic for DeAndre. We held up our glasses and lightly clinked the rims together. DeAndre's eyes met mine as our glasses touched, but then he quickly looked away. My body stiffened as I shifted in my seat. He appeared to be observing the space, his eyes sweeping around the large room, and I smiled at him expectantly. My grin widened as I waited for his gaze to land on me. He took a sip of his drink and then looked back up at the TV. The corners of my lips fell and I could feel my cheeks get hot.

I looked down at my hands and nervously picked at my mahogany nail polish, searching my brain for something to talk about. "How's work?" I asked.

"It's good," he said. He took another sip without taking his eyes off the TV.

"Is something wrong?" I asked. I tried not to sound annoyed, but my patience was waning.

He shook his head.

If we were at home, I would have said, "Don't lie to me. I know you." And I'd continue to poke, wearing him down until he finally told me what was wrong. Maybe it would turn into an argument, but I wouldn't care because there was nothing more frustrating to me than a one-sided attempt at conflict resolution. We'd agreed long ago, though, to never argue in public. This rule was new to me at the time—in past relationships, I never hesitated to have a screaming match on a busy sidewalk if the circumstances angered me enough. I raised my voice at DeAndre in public one time during a disagreement, a few months into our relationship. He leaned in and said calmly, "Mary, I don't do this." Since then, I cherished our mutual promise to never quarrel in front of an audience.

The waitress set our food on the table. "Need anything else right now?" she asked.

"No, thank you," DeAndre and I said in unison.

I shoved forkfuls of chopped asparagus into my mouth, hardly chewing long enough to enjoy it. My eyes dampened, and I blinked quickly to keep my tears from pooling and falling into my salad. When I finished eating, I pushed my plate forward a few inches and sat back in my chair with my arms crossed. I looked around the restaurant at other groups of people—couples sitting nearby immersed in conversation—and I plunged deeper into humiliation.

"Any dessert?" the waitress asked.

I looked at DeAndre. He usually left this decision to me, and it was almost always an emphatic "yes!"

"Just the check, please," he said.

The waitress set our bill on the table, and DeAndre reached for it. I stood out of my seat, swung my purse over my shoulder, and walked toward the door. Outside, I stood at the edge of the sidewalk with my arms crossed and my jaw clenched, exhaling sharply through my nose like a raging bull. DeAndre walked out of the restaurant a few minutes later and looked at me. Our eyes were locked for a moment.

"Oh, so you can see me," I snapped.

His shoulders dropped and he shook his head as he turned to walk toward our apartment building.

I stepped toward him and leaned in close. "What the fuck did I do? What's wrong with you? Talk to me!" I begged.

He turned quickly to face me. "How am I supposed to feel, Mary? How do you expect me to feel today?" His eyes widened, and we stared at each other, our bodies statues on the busy street. His words were heavy, hitting me in the center of my chest.

"Oh, fuck," I said. I dropped my arms and softened my scowl. I looked down at my feet. My whole body was warm, my hands clammy as shame pulsed through me. What was I doing?

We couldn't mask this day with pink lipstick and high heels, charcuterie boards and top-shelf liquor. This wasn't a rom-com, and I couldn't expect to flirt our feelings away with a half-assed impersonation of Drew Barrymore on a date. This was our real life, and in real life, our hearts were fucking broken. I was an asshole for suggesting we distort our reality into a PG-13 movie, like throwing a sparkly, sequin tarp over our raw, bloody wounds. My eyes filled with tears as I opened my mouth to apologize.

"You're right. I wasn't thinking," I said. I dabbed the corners of my eyes with my fingertips and caught my tears before they could leave rivers of black mascara on my cheeks.

DeAndre reached his hand out. I grabbed it and stepped toward him.

"Come on, let's go get dessert," he said. He led us down the street to a cafe that served more than a dozen types of pie by the slice and ordered two slices of cherry pie to-go.

When we got home, I kicked off my heels and changed into a soft T-shirt and sweatpants. DeAndre turned on the TV, and we sat on the couch and scooped gobs of gooey cherries and thick, sugary pie crust into our mouths. I set the empty clamshell container on the coffee table and scooted a few inches closer to DeAndre. He put his fork down and rested his hand on top of mine.

* * *

Over the next few weeks, the anxious flutters in my belly returned, growing more pronounced every day that passed. When someone walked by pushing a baby stroller, or when I heard light footsteps sprinting down the hallway outside of our apartment door, my heart overflowed. I was ready to start trying for a baby again, but my overwhelming desire was eclipsed by sheer terror. *What if we have another miscarriage?* I asked myself this question every time I imagined becoming pregnant again. The answer was always the same: another miscarriage will kill me.

With DeAndre's blessing, I made an appointment with a Reproductive Endocrinologist, and at the end of November, we had our consultation with Dr. Goldstein. She was upbeat as she explained every potential problem she would be looking for—phase one involved blood tests for us both and one humbling semen analysis for DeAndre.

We returned to Dr. Goldstein's office a week later and sat across from her as she pulled up our test results on her computer.

"Everything looks normal so far, but DeAndre, your sperm count came back low. I'm a little baffled by this since you've had no issues getting pregnant. It might be good to retest you in a few months. If you felt nervous, it could have affected the results," she said.

I turned and glanced at DeAndre. He was biting his lower lip and nodding along. His hands were resting in his lap, and I wanted to reach over and put my hand on his forearm, commiserate with a small gesture as he'd often done for me. I knew he'd despise the attention at that moment, though, so I looked away from him and back to the doctor.

"I want to do a saline ultrasound on you, Mary, to check for a uterine septum," Dr. Goldstein continued. She started drawing a rough doodle of a uterus on a piece of paper. "In some women, the uterus doesn't finish developing, and they're born with this anomaly, extra tissue that partially divides the uterus. This is a common cause of recurrent miscarriages. If this is the case, the good news is that we can easily correct it with surgery." She drew a curved shape down the middle of the uterus and scribbled it in.

A nurse led us into a large exam room for the ultrasound. As I lay on the exam table with a cloth sheet over my bare thighs, Dr. Goldstein slowly filled my uterus with a saline solution through a long, narrow tube. The inside of my abdomen felt ice cold. Cramps pinched and pulled as my uterus expanded like a water balloon. When my uterine cavity was full, she began the ultrasound, moving the wand around slowly as she stared at the screen. Something caught her attention, and she held the wand in place.

"See that," she said.

I nodded, but I couldn't see anything notable on the screen.

She lost the image and tried to get it back in view but couldn't. "It looks like you might have a small septum. I want you to get a pelvic MRI to confirm."

* * *

DeAndre drove me to my pelvic scan on an early, rainy December morning. On our way home after the 20-minute appointment, we stopped for coffee, our treat for being up and out the door before 8 a.m. We drove out of the Starbucks parking lot, and as I took a sip of my almond milk latte, my phone rang.

"Mary, it's Dr. Goldstein. I got your scan results. You have a pretty large septum in your uterus!" she said.

"Oh, wow. What does this mean?" I asked.

"Well, it's good that we found it because we can assume most, if not all of your miscarriages were a result of you having this septum. And as I said before, we can correct it with a simple procedure. I'm going to refer you to a surgeon to get that scheduled."

I immediately began raking the internet to find out more details about my uterine anomaly. I read about women who had relatively healthy pregnancies with a septum, though this was extremely rare. In almost all cases, including mine, the septum tissue is located in prime implantation territory. Though it presents like normal uterine lining, it isn't a reliable source of nourishment for a fetus. This explained why my first and third pregnancies ended at almost the exact same gestational period, just one day apart. My septum only allowed enough blood supply to sustain a pregnancy through the sixth week. At that point, even though the fetuses were seemingly healthy, they died.

We'd been climbing up this steep hill for a year, the top becoming farther away with every pregnancy and subsequent loss. Now we were almost there, and it was our turn to run, screaming and rejoicing, down the other side. No more cradling debilitating fear, resting in the crook of my elbow and taking up space that belongs to my child. No more protecting my heart from falling too deeply in love with a delicate dream, only to have it ripped away.

I called to schedule our consultation with the surgeon, and his earliest opening was the first week of January. While on the phone with the nurse, she said, "We need to get the procedure scheduled now, as well. He can do February 14th. Does that work for you?"

Valentine's Day, and my late grandmother's birthday. I thought this must be a message from her. Three months ago, I called my mom crying after our last miscarriage. She said to me as she fought back tears, "I think grandma is taking good care of your babies." Her words struck me, and I sobbed harder. I didn't know where their spirits went after they left us. Was there a spiritual orphanage in another realm, a glowing sandbox with all the spirits of babies we'd loved and lost? I wasn't sure what I believed, but I liked my mom's suggestion. If they're with my grandmother, they will always know love.

"Yes," I said to the nurse. "February 14th is perfect."

*   *   *

As Christmas lights went up around the city and holiday movies began airing nightly across every network, our home felt increasingly dreary. The corner of our living room, where I'd once imagined a Christmas tree would go —towering over shiny wrapped gifts with oversized bows —was empty. Holiday cheer didn't live in this space where beige carpet came together with white walls in every corner, and when I looked around our apartment, I sank deeper into despair.

"Should we get a small Christmas tree?" I asked DeAndre.

"Yeah, we can do that," he said. He raised his eyebrows slightly and nodded in agreement.

We went to Target that night to browse the miniature artificial Christmas trees—just a pinch of holiday spirit to liven up the mood in our home. We turned corners in the brightly lit maze, looking for big red signs pointing us in the right direction. We passed through aisles of baby clothes, petite outfits dangling from plastic hangers, plush toys and pacifiers, baby bathtubs, and yellow rubber duckies whose painted eyes followed us through the aisle. Stacks of diapers with photos of giggling babies towered over us on both sides. I walked faster and turned the corner.

We circled the Christmas tree displays—half-empty now that it was mid-December—and searched the bare shelves for a three-foot-tall tree in a box. I heard a child's voice, and I turned toward the sound. A woman pushed her cart past the aisle. A small child trailed behind her, struggling to carry a toy too big for her arms. It was such an ordinary moment, but it punctured my spirit.

I watched the woman and child walk out of view, and my chin began to quiver.

"Let's leave," I said.

DeAndre and I left the store and walked through the parking lot to our car. We sat for a moment in the darkness, our silhouettes illuminated by yellow light shining on us from the lamppost above. He turned to me, and I could feel his stare, studying me while I wiped away tears.

"We should have baby things to wrap and put under the tree, but we don't because our baby isn't here. I hate this. It isn't fair," I said.

DeAndre reached over and curled his fingers around mine. "I hate it too," he said.

* * *

Instead of sulking in our lackluster apartment, absent of bright red stockings, fresh pine needles falling on a plaid tree skirt, and mistletoe dangling above the entryway, we decided to escape it. We booked a last-minute trip to Las Vegas for the week of Christmas. It was the ideal family-*un*friendly destination.

Our friends with small children spent the week telling imaginative stories of Santa and his reindeer, watching their sweet children unwrap new toys on their living room floor, and cooking up a holiday feast for the whole family. Meanwhile, DeAndre and I stayed out every night until the early morning hours, gambling, eating out at overpriced hotel restaurants, and drinking cocktails to our hearts' content, dazzled by bright lights and the hypnotic chimes of spinning slot machines.

I woke up around 5 a.m. on our last morning in Vegas, overcome with nausea. I jumped out of bed, rushed to the bathroom, and threw up. When I came out of the bathroom, DeAndre rolled over and looked at me, concerned.

"You're not pregnant, are you?" he asked.

"Ha. Yeah right. There's no way in hell," I said.

My hair smelled like smoke from the casinos. The bile I'd just puked up tasted like ash. I wasn't the least bit surprised that the disgusting combination of secondhand smoke and alcohol made me ill.

* * *

We spent New Year's Eve at home in L.A., sipping pink Prosecco and flipping through various New Year's Eve broadcasts on TV. I fought heavy eyelids as the ball dropped at midnight, and nudged DeAndre, who had already fallen asleep on the couch, to wake up and watch the last seconds of the New Year's Eve countdown. We shared a brief kiss at midnight, turned off the TV, and went to bed.

I slept late into the morning on January 1st and dragged myself to the kitchen to make coffee—a typical Sunday. I curled up on the couch under a gray woven blanket, where I sipped my coffee for the next hour. I spent the remainder of the day watching TV until the golden evening light faded, and the sky outside darkened.

I twitched my nose involuntarily. Something was bothering me, and I sat up.

"What is that smell?" I mumbled to myself. I waved my hand in front of my face. "Why does it smell like coffee in here?" I reached for my mug on the coffee table and looked inside. A thin layer of residue glistened along the curved edge at the bottom, the aroma smacking me in the face as I raised the mug to my nose.

"Oh no," I said under my breath. I opened the cycle tracking app on my phone. I wasn't tracking my cycle as diligently, but with my surgery approaching, I had begun taking my temperature again and charting the results to pinpoint when I was fertile so we could use protection or avoid sex altogether on the days leading up to ovulation. My period was three days late.

I rationalized as my heart raced. *Lots of things can delay a period. It's been a stressful month. I had that saline ultrasound, which probably threw things off-kilter. Lack of sleep, late nights out drinking in Vegas. My body is just out of whack.*

I calmed down as I talked myself into believing this story. Still, I had to know for sure. Sensitivity to smells was a pregnancy symptom I'd had in the past.

I went into the bathroom and pulled a test from my stash under the sink. I peed on it, replaced the plastic cap, and set the test on the back of the toilet. I checked the time so I could return in three minutes to see the results. There was an anecdote among my friends that the quickest way to get your period to come is to take a pregnancy test. My body was relaxed, my mind already at ease as I walked back into the bathroom to check the test. *My period will probably arrive in the next five minutes, and*

I'll have wasted this test for nothing, I thought. I saw the results as I stepped through the doorway.

"You have got to be kidding me," I said.

I started weeping as I came out of the bathroom holding the test. I dropped it on the ledge that separated the kitchen from the living room. I leaned my elbows on the ledge, put my hands over my face, and sobbed. DeAndre was sitting at his desk with his back to me. He took off his headphones and turned around.

"What's wrong?" he asked. He looked bewildered as he stood from his seat and walked toward me.

I parted my hands to reveal my face, cheeks wet with tears, and said, "I'm pregnant."

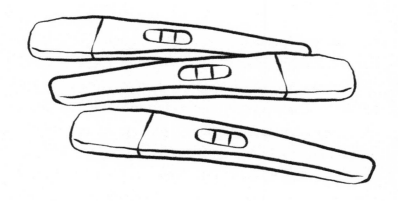

landmines

DeAndre wrapped his arms around me as I wiped my wet face with my shirt. My mind was racing, my thoughts colliding into each other like a five-car pile-up on the freeway. *We'll have another miscarriage, I'm sure of it. Dr. Goldstein is going to be annoyed with us. Maybe I should terminate. Fuck, how could this happen?*

DeAndre dropped his arms and stepped back. He picked up the test and stared at it for a few seconds, then placed it back on the countertop. I wondered if he was pissed at me for not being more attentive to my cycle.

"I *knew* I didn't have a low sperm count! That test was bullshit!" he shouted. He was smiling, and his over the moon reaction startled me. The stream of conflicting emotions coming from both of us almost knocked me off balance. I snapped out of shock and burst into loud, unrestrained laughter.

The next day, I called Dr. Goldstein, nervous to tell her as if she was going to put us in timeout like a couple of misbehaving kids. I chewed on my thumbnail as I waited to hear her reaction.

"Well, let's be cautiously optimistic! Your septum is very, very small," she assured me. I remembered a month ago when she told me it was large, but I put that out of my mind—if Dr. Goldstein had confidence in this pregnancy, then I would too.

I spent every mundane moment thinking about all the ways this could go right. I questioned why our journey was taking this turn, and I started to rewrite the story as my optimism bloomed. It is called the *miracle of life*, after all.

* * *

Dr. Goldstein encouraged us to keep our appointment with the surgeon, Dr. Munro, the following week to learn more about my uterine septum. Dr. Munro reminded me of a fun-loving dad that you see in movies—a Robin Williams type—with shaggy salt and pepper hair that hung over his forehead. His pleasant demeanor offered a soft place to land as I struggled with the mortifying reality that we couldn't adhere to the only rule we'd been given leading up to my surgery: don't get pregnant.

"So, I hear you got pregnant unexpectedly!" he said.

"Yeah… oops." My face warmed, blushing bright pink.

Dr. Munro wheeled a stool over and sat down to face us. "Well, it's not impossible to have a baby with a uterine septum. It all depends if the embryo has implanted itself in the septum tissue or another part of the uterine wall. The biggest concern is the baby running out of space, which would result in giving birth prematurely. If you want, I can do an ultrasound today and see how things are looking," he said.

"That would be amazing," I said. I leaned back on the exam table and rested my heels in the stirrups.

"You're about five weeks along. There's the baby," he said, pointing to a pea-sized dot on the screen. "And there's your septum." He traced his finger around a light gray triangle at the top center of my uterus.

"Can you tell if it's implanted in the septum?" I asked, straining my neck to get a better view.

He stared at the screen for a few moments as he moved the ultrasound probe around. "It's too early to tell, but everything looks good otherwise," he said. He rolled his chair back and removed his gloves. "I'll leave *you three* to get dressed." He smiled as he handed us the sonogram printout before he left the room.

I sat up and studied the sonogram, noting where the septum was in relation to the fetus. I ran my finger over the space between the two shapes. The fetus sat several centimeters away from it. In the image in my hand, they weren't even touching. My confidence warped into arrogance. Dr. Munro couldn't see it, but I could—this baby was going to make it.

* * *

Dr. Goldstein stepped into the exam room where DeAndre and I were waiting with lumps in our throats.

"So much for low sperm count, huh?" she said.

DeAndre and I laughed as I scooted to the edge of the exam table for our six-week ultrasound. I squeezed his hand just as I did the first time we heard our baby's heartbeat 11 months ago, but it wasn't the same. The tender pitter-patter was not accompanied by the familiar rush of adrenaline, the trickling of happy tears. There was only temporary relief as we anticipated our next appointment. We'd never seen life at seven weeks.

"I'm going to be away next week, so you can see another doctor or wait until the following week," Dr. Goldstein said.

I thought about how I wanted to be with Dr. Goldstein if we were to get bad news, but I quickly shook that idea out of my mind, unwilling to give it my attention. There was no more loss on the horizon for us. Only miracles.

* * *

Later that week, I flew to New York City to visit Gretchen. We had planned this trip on impulse after the presidential election in November, to drive to Washington D.C. for the Women's March. I'd shared a handful of poster designs on my Instagram page after the election—emphasizing the collective rage of everyone I knew—and people started messaging me from all over the country asking if they could print them out to carry as signs at their local marches.

I made the posters available to download on Etsy, and I saw at least a dozen people carrying them during the march. Friends sent me pictures of people carrying my signs in their hometowns. I saw candid photos of a purple poster I'd illustrated—with frilly underwear that read "Keep Your Filthy Laws Off My Silky Drawers"—displayed front and center on pop culture pages and social media news sites. It was the first time I'd felt so many eyes on my art.

As we walked along the National Mall, I envisioned a few years down the road, showing my child pictures we'd taken that weekend—among a sea of hundreds of thousands of people marching in opposition to the new administration—marking their earliest days nestled safely in mommy's belly.

* * *

The day after I returned home, DeAndre and I met with a different doctor to have my seven-week ultrasound. The ultrasound was business as usual—the doctor measured and pointed out the sac and fetus. I nodded along, resisting my urge to gesture with my hand for her to speed it up, get to the good part already.

"Hmm. I can't find a heartbeat," she said. Her tone was flat, and she seemed indifferent, uncaring. I clenched my jaw and blinked a bunch of times, fighting against the warm pools rising in my eyes. The doctor was icy, and my tears were not safe with her.

I wondered if I'd done something wrong by traveling, by being on my feet all day in Washington, D.C. I thought further back to Las Vegas, before I knew I was pregnant. Did I do irreversible damage to this shadow of life by having mimosas with breakfast and inhaling thick clouds of secondhand smoke? I knew better than to blame myself. I'd collected stories from friends who found out they were pregnant after a cocaine binge or a week of heavy drinking. Living, breathing children were always at the end of these stories. That wouldn't be my story, though, not this time.

* * *

Grief's cold familiar arms embraced us as we crossed the threshold into our apartment. I slipped off my shoes by the entryway with heaviness in my heart, the solemn silence in our home magnified by the news we'd just received.

"Do you want me to text everyone?" I asked.

DeAndre nodded.

We had only told a few people about our accidental pregnancy, once believed to be our magical, miracle baby, but sending even one text stifled my breath and made my face pink with fever. I was the cause of this chain reaction, pulling our loved ones into the shadows to collectively mourn yet again.

DeAndre and I didn't talk about it, or anything really, for the rest of the day—we didn't need to. We were mirrors, reflecting the sharp edges of our broken hearts every time our eyes met.

DeAndre tapped my arm lightly the next morning as I sat with my knees curled into my chest and my head resting on the armrest of our couch. I looked up at him standing above me. He said, "I just need to say that I'm sad."

* * *

Valium surged through my body as we arrived for my D&C appointment. A rush of euphoria swirled inside me, masking any physical discomfort as my body became numb from the inside out.

The procedure was quick, or perhaps I'd just drifted somewhere above the clouds until it was over, because I don't remember any of it except for the doctor rubbing my knee gently as she said, "We're all done, Mary. Take your time getting dressed." Her voice was so kind. I wanted to reach my arms out and embrace her. I'd close my eyes and pretend she was my mom or my sister, and I'd let my tears fall onto the shoulder of her white coat as she rubbed my back.

I spent a few minutes alone in the exam room, lying down as I waited for the lightheadedness to fade. I stood up and carefully pulled on my soft black jersey pants. I slid my feet into my red sneakers and kneeled down to tie the laces.

I opened the door to leave and found a nurse waiting for me in the hall. I walked out and steadied myself on the wall. The nurse stayed at my side with her fingers wrapped loosely around my upper arm as she walked me out to the waiting room. She pushed the door open, and I saw DeAndre sitting front and center. He looked up at me, and his eyes felt like home. I sat down next to him and rested my head on his shoulder. He held my hand, and I closed my eyes to savor a rare moment of peaceful surrender.

* * *

I was recovering at home two days later when my phone buzzed with text messages from friends. Beyoncé had just announced her pregnancy—twins! The news exploded everywhere, including my text message inbox. Most of my friends didn't know what I had just been through. Some knew but got carried away with Beyoncé's viral announcement that they momentarily forgot, and who could blame them? Under normal circumstances, I'd be the first person to fire off a series of Beyoncé-related texts in all-caps to everyone I know. These weren't normal circumstances, though, and I wanted to throw my phone out the window.

I replied: *I had my fourth miscarriage a few days ago, so I can't talk about this right now. Sorry.*

My phone rang immediately, but I declined their calls. I didn't think I'd be able to speak or even hear my friends' voices without crumbling.

My phone rang again a minute later, and I recognized the number as the surgeon's office. I quickly pulled myself together and answered.

"Hi Mary, we heard about your loss. I'm so sorry," the nurse said. "Dr. Munro wanted me to call and reschedule your surgery. He has May 11th available."

I looked at my calendar. May felt so, so far away. "Yes, that works. I'll take it," I said.

"Okay. I'm calling in your prescriptions, which you need to start four weeks before surgery," she said. Then her voice softened, and she asked, "How are you feeling?"

"I'm fine." My voice cracked, and I started sobbing. "Sorry, I'm just... it just hurts. Thank you for asking."

* * *

I envied people who could easily be online, scroll social media unconcerned about whether they'd step on a landmine as their thumb moved up and down the screen. What is it like to scroll past pregnancy announcements, baby showers, and first birthday parties without a racing heart and a lump in your throat? I wondered if people were aware that their sweet, shared moments could blow some of us to pieces.

DeAndre was driving us home from the store one afternoon while I sat in the passenger seat, scrolling Facebook on my phone. A sonogram picture appeared in my feed, an acquaintance who I'd never met in-person announcing she was pregnant. I set my phone in my lap and looked out the window. My lower lip quivered, and I pulled on it with my teeth. I observed people outside— teenagers waiting for the bus, a mother carrying grocery bags alongside a small child holding an unkempt doll in their arms—and imagined what their day was like, writing stories about them in my mind to distract from the ache in my chest.

"Why are you so quiet?" DeAndre asked.

I shook my head.

"Babe," he said. "What's wrong? Come on, I know you."

I whimpered, trying to hold it in as I shook my head again. I could feel DeAndre staring at me as we waited at a red light, and I started bawling, not bothering to look for a tissue or catch the tears with my fingertips. "I just saw a pregnancy announcement on Facebook," I said. "They're so fucking painful sometimes."

DeAndre reached over and rubbed my forearm. "Aw, I understand. Who is it?" he asked.

"That's the thing, I don't even know her! It doesn't make any fucking sense!"

After witnessing me unravel over that Facebook post, DeAndre treaded lightly around the topic. He would tell me, ever so delicately, "You know my friend Alex? His wife is pregnant. Sorry, I hope that doesn't upset you."

"Aww," I'd say. "That's so great."

I didn't linger here too long, trying to understand why some pregnancy announcements sent me into a tailspin while others rolled right off me. I was just grateful to make it through another announcement in one piece.

Every reaction of mine set the tone for the next announcement. Since I was unfazed by the most recent pregnancy news, DeAndre loosened up, my fragile eggshell exterior breaking under the weight of his words.

"Oh, by the way, Katie is pregnant," he blurted out one day, referring to a mutual friend of ours.

I froze as I felt my heart explode. An avalanche of tears followed.

"Oh shit, I'm sorry," DeAndre said. After I collected myself, he said, with more caution this time, "I don't want this to come out the wrong way. Can I ask you how come you get really upset sometimes when you find out someone is pregnant, and other times you're okay?"

I thought for a minute. "I have no idea," I sighed.

On my birthday the year before, I saw a friend's pregnancy announcement on Facebook. I'd found out weeks earlier through the grapevine that she was pregnant, but she hadn't shared it publicly. I opened Facebook to read my birthday notifications, as one does, and I saw the sonogram photo at the top of my feed. I closed the app and tossed my phone to the other side of the couch.

DeAndre found me a few minutes later, weeping on the couch. "Whoa, what happened?!" he asked.

I opened Facebook and showed him the post. "On my fucking birthday?! Seriously?!"

DeAndre gave me space to cry that day, and we pushed it aside. When I brought it up later, still bothered by it, he said, "You know, she didn't do that to hurt you. I'm sure she didn't even realize it was your birthday when she posted it."

I was so far gone by that point. You couldn't convince me that every pregnancy announcement wasn't designed to break me. You couldn't convince me that the origins of public pregnancy announcements weren't malicious, that their celebrations weren't designed to rub salt in the wounds of those who longed to cradle a bump behind a black and white profile of their baby's body with a letter board spelling out the month of their expected arrival—a minefield to so many.

Still, I tried really hard. I pressed that fucking *Like* button and double-tapped until the heart turned red, before logging off and tending to my own heart, repeatedly bruised by my naive willingness to participate in the era of social media.

As my friends got pregnant with their first, second, third babies, they'd send me private messages. They all followed the same template:

> *Hey, I wanted to let you know that I'm pregnant. I'll probably post an announcement next week, but I wanted to tell you first, so you're not devastated when you see it.*

I wondered if I had it backward, if perhaps *I* was the landmine that everyone else feared.

Through watching friends and relatives take turns having babies, I got very good at checking my pain at the door. It was my duty to make sure that my suffering didn't become tangled up in their joy. Keeping this up was sometimes agonizing, and a few times, it meant I had to skip the baby shower or first birthday party.

The tears I shed while scrolling social media were never about a pregnancy announcement nor the person sharing their joy. My tears poured out of me because when I looked at their sonogram photo propped up behind a pair of baby shoes, I am reminded that our child should be three-months-old now, or nine-months-old, or 18-months-old with a sibling on the way. I am reminded that I never got to kiss their soft heads or hum lullabies while I rock them to sleep in a dark nursery illuminated only by moonlight. I am reminded of all the memories we never had a chance to create because they left us so soon.

spirits

DeAndre sat in a chair next to me as I lay reclined on the exam table, my legs covered with thick white blankets, and blue hospital booties pulled over my pale pink floral socks. Dr. Munro cut away the septum tissue while projecting the entire procedure, from the inside of my uterus, on a large flatscreen monitor hanging above my head. My insides were numb, but I could feel pressure and dull poking as he navigated the area. I twisted my neck to look up as I watched him cauterize the pink flesh inside my womb while my mouth filled with an intense taste of burnt almonds. Dr. Munro warned me this might happen, but only after it already started and I was about to shout that I thought my insides were on fire.

When the surgery was over, my whole body shivered and my teeth chattered like a wind-up toy, a side effect from the anesthesia. I wrapped my arms around myself, trying to still my trembling limbs. Dr. Munro handed me a printout, a set of four full-color photos taken from inside my uterus during the procedure. They were just blurry, indistinguishable pink and white shapes, but I smiled as I studied the images—they represented the end of a harrowing chapter.

It would be a few months before Dr. Munro would give us the green light to get pregnant again. I wanted to spend that time preparing, just as I had done two years ago when I threw out my birth control and devoured every recommended book on fertility and conception. I missed the innocence of that time, when a positive pregnancy test was met with excitement and awe because it meant that life was going to change forever—it would never be just the two of us again. Though, to be fair, life had been changed forever by that first positive pregnancy test—it initiated us into this dreadful club that no one wishes to be a part of.

Dr. Goldstein shared promising statistics with us after my uterine septum was diagnosed. She showed us charts and graphs explaining our odds of giving birth after one, two, three, four miscarriages—the number dramatically decreasing. But, she explained, now that we had a cause, and more importantly, a cure, I was practically as good as new.

This didn't feel like a clean slate, though. There weren't enough glowing statistics in existence that would stop my stomach from flipping or my heart from racing at the thought of being pregnant again. My miscarriages robbed me of the naive joy that is awarded to pregnancies absent of heartbreak. As my womb healed from surgery, my heart was heavy, burdened by residual trauma from four consecutive losses.

* * *

Rosie and Alyssa raved to me on multiple occasions that summer about a psychic medium they'd both seen recently. They'd gotten insight into their careers, relationships, past and future circumstances, and they'd received enlightening spiritual advice during their sessions. When I shared that I was hoping to heal some of my miscarriage trauma before trying to get pregnant again, Rosie and Alyssa both said to me, "You should get a reading with Kira. You'll love her." Moved by their glowing reviews, I booked a 30-minute reading with Kira in July.

Kira's space was on the second floor of an apothecary in North Hollywood. The room was the size of a small office, with a square table draped in a dark purple tablecloth and a chair on either side. There were mystical posters on the wall—nighttime nature dreamscapes and illustrated moon phases. Ribbons of earthy, sweet-smelling smoke snaked toward the window from a stick of incense that had just finished burning. I didn't provide any backstory, only introduced myself as I sat down across from her. She laid out Tarot cards on the table in front of her.

"Have you been trying to grow your family?" she asked.

"Yes," I nodded.

She furrowed her brows, then opened her mouth, but hesitated to speak for a moment. "When you lose a pregnancy, no matter the circumstances, you're only losing the body. That's the part that dies. Their spirits don't die. They can return to you another time," she said.

My heart swelled. "I've had four miscarriages," I said. "We're going to start trying again."

"Ah, okay," she said. She looked satisfied as if she'd solved a riddle. She shuffled her Tarot cards again and laid several out in a row. Her expression became focused. "Two children are coming through. I'm getting the message that it wasn't the right body or the right time for them. They seem to be unsure about which one should be born first," she said with a smirk.

I laughed as my eyes became wet. I dabbed my tears with a tissue as Kira continued to speak.

"There is an energetic block in your sacral chakra, your womb area." She paused again. She looked as if she was listening to someone speak as she moved her pen quickly across a page in her notebook. "Get a white candle, maybe with Gardenia essence, and set it in water. Also, a piece of orange fruit, something juicy," she said. Her fingers curled as if she was holding an invisible tennis ball. "A peach. Get a peach, pray over it with your intentions, and bury it. Think of it like planting a seed for what you want to see grow," she said.

I nodded along as she prescribed my spiritual homework, all of it so far out of the ordinary as if she was instructing me in a foreign language. Yet I felt myself opening, my petals curling outward. I was eager to go home and follow her suggestions.

"Your guides want to help you with this," Kira said. "You have a lot of support." She paused, focusing intently, and then she smiled. "My great grandmother is coming through for you. She's saying she wants to help. Her name is Dove." Kira looked surprised as she delivered this information with a smile. "Talk to Dove anytime, she's here to help you!"

I smiled, touched by the unseen gesture—a team of spirit guides rallying around to help shepherd me into motherhood.

At the end of the session, Kira hugged me. "Remember, you can always ask your guides for help. They want to help you," she said.

I left the room breathless, as though I'd just spent the last half hour jogging around the block in the valley summer heat. I imbibed Kira's messages—together, they were a cocktail of heartache and unexpected relief. *Their spirits don't die. They can return to you another time.* I repeated these words, weaving together and wrapping around my body like a warm blanket.

I'd wrestled with my beliefs around losing a baby. I often wondered if we'd lost four siblings, one after the other falling away like crackling brown leaves in October, their spirits gone forever. That's how I'd often read about miscarriage—a loss as permanent as death. I'd read about babies lost in the womb who were given names, and sometimes memorial sites, if only a heart-shaped rock placed among flowers in the backyard.

It soothed me to see the different ways people coped with this sudden death before birth, a delicate new life vanishing in an instant. I'd learned that there are no defined rules, and we get to decide our truths. As I walked out of my reading with Kira, her words replaced every story I'd struggled to write around my miscarriages.

Our babies were with us—perhaps whispering to us through a tiny orb of light in a photograph, a butterfly dancing across my path, or a small white feather stuck to the windshield of our car. They hadn't died; they just needed more time. On occasions, I would talk to them when I was alone. "I miss you," I'd say. Sometimes, when I couldn't sleep, I'd press my cheek into my pillow and whisper, "I love you. I can't wait for you to get here."

* * *

I ordered a white Gardenia candle off the internet and placed it on my nightstand, allowing the floral scent to decorate the air in our bedroom for a few hours each day. I bought a ripe peach at the grocery store and put it in my backpack. I wrapped it in a few layers of paper towels to keep it from getting pierced by my laptop case and sketchbooks. As I took the metro to my new job— designing part-time for a hemp snack food startup in West L.A.—and back home, including a short walk on both ends of my commute, I looked for an appropriate place to bury my peach. We didn't have a yard, and I wasn't going to dig up dirt on someone else's property or in a park where the ground was packed solid and impossible to penetrate—full disclosure, though, I *did* try that once.

The peach had been rolling around in my bag for two days and was soft with bruises. After I got home from work late in the afternoon, I quietly slid the back door open and tiptoed from our bedroom out onto our small patio. I stayed far to one side, so DeAndre wouldn't catch me through the living room window doing some weird shit that I didn't know how to explain, and I examined the landscaping. A large plot of soil surrounded our ground floor concrete patio. The plot was level with the patio wall, about chest-height, and lined with two rows of small shrubs. I touched the dirt with my fingertips. It was damp and loose—in other words, easy to dig.

"That'll do," I said to myself. I carefully scooped out a handful of soil without disturbing the plants. I placed my peach in the shallow hole and covered it back up. As I patted the dirt, I silently asked my guides for assistance with fertility, a smooth pregnancy, and a sweet baby in my arms. I went back inside to wash the thick, dark soil caked under my fingernails.

I called my friend Jacqueline to tell her about my reading with Kira and all the rituals she had prescribed me. I knew Jacqueline would welcome these stories—this sort of thing was the norm for her. Like Alyssa, Jacqueline would often remind me when it was a new moon or full moon, even though I still didn't really understand what any of it meant. She'd often keep me up to speed on astrological current events and explain how they might affect me. She was also an expert in plant medicine.

Jacqueline and I first met as young art school students 16 years ago, where we bonded over teenage crushes and spent every Saturday night during the summer dancing to 80s music at The Ruby, an 18-and-over club in Hollywood. Now, what felt like many lifetimes later, and with the help of Facebook, Jacqueline and I were growing close again after years of being out of touch with one another. I often wondered if our paths crossed again so that Jacqueline could impart her wisdom upon me, as I now half-jokingly referred to her as my spiritual tutor.

"The psychic told me my sacral chakra is blocked," I told her over the phone.

"Girl, that's your womb!" Jacqueline said.

"Help! How the hell do I fix this?"

"You should start working with herbal infusions," she said. "Here, I'm gonna talk you through it. Write this down."

I typed frantically in my notes app while she shared herbal infusion recipes I could make at home. She explained the healing properties of each recommended herb. Schisandra berries will create movement. Dried rose petals will open my heart and encourage self-love. Jasmine will help me soften. Red raspberry leaf will ground me.

"Infusions are strong herbal medicine," she told me. "Sit in a quiet place and spend a few minutes drinking them in the morning while you meditate. Visualize your womb as a golden chalice. Right now, the waters are stagnant. When you drink the infusions, the medicine will flow into your chalice and create a whirlpool."

I'd heard enough. I was ready to shake up my chalice waters. Jacqueline referred me to a trusted botanical company, and my first order of herbs arrived in the mail a few days later.

I lined up two mason jars on the kitchen counter. I put a small handful of dried herbs in each jar and filled them with hot water to steep overnight, my new evening ritual. In the morning, I grabbed one jar from the kitchen counter and poured the liquid through a strainer into a clean glass. I brought the glass—filled to the rim with pinkish clear liquid—back to bed. I sat in bed with my eyes closed and sipped, letting the tart, floral liquid flow past my lips. When my cup was empty, I opened my journal and scribbled my thoughts, fears, and dreams onto the pages.

Every day that I devoted even the smallest window of time to my spiritual healing, I craved more—more exercises to nourish my healing efforts, more spiritual tools that I never would have imagined seeking out until now.

* * *

That summer, I started following a blogger on Instagram who shared openly that she had suffered two miscarriages. She was six months pregnant, and her raw vulnerability about being pregnant after miscarriage offered a sense of hope that I struggled to find within myself. I visited her blog to drink in more of her words as if they were supplemental medicine for my healing. She shared how she used crystals to support her fertility and assist in overcoming the trauma of her miscarriages. My heart and mind now cracked wide open, I made a list of each crystal she recommended, and after work one day, I went on a field trip to a spiritual shop in Santa Monica.

The shop was two-stories with a bookstore upstairs. On the ground floor, oracle and Tarot decks lined shelves on the wall behind tables displaying incense, beaded jewelry, and candles. Tapestries hung overhead, and meditation pillows were piled neatly in one corner. A large area of the shop was dedicated to crystals. Little mountains of stones in every color sat in bowls on the shelves and tables.

I pulled out my list and plucked a few choice crystals out of their bowls. Carnelian was at the top of my list, a smooth, dark orange stone known to support the sacral chakra. I picked out a small, jagged-edged purple amethyst to help relieve stress and anxiety, and a cotton candy pink rose quartz to open my heart. I selected two small white moonstone crystals, each no larger than a Peanut M&M, to enhance fertility. For protection from miscarriage, I picked up a garnet stone, and for absorbing negative energy, black tourmaline. My hands were full as I carried my crystals to the register. They clinked into each other like pieces of hard candy as I set them on the glass countertop.

When I got home, I laid my new crystals out on the bed and revisited the blogger's website, where she'd included a step-by-step guide to caring for crystals. The first step was cleansing and dedicating each one—in other words, clean old energy off them and convey how you'd like them to help you. I held each of my new crystals under running water and, one-by-one, dedicated an intention, much like making a wish before blowing out birthday candles.

I read her blog further and learned that it's good practice to energetically charge your crystals by putting them outside or near a window on every full moon. I googled the next full moon and set a calendar reminder in my phone. Pleased with my work, I arranged my crystals on my nightstand.

Though I felt much more grounded as I continued to pick up new habits that supported my healing, I couldn't shake the underlying panic from Kira telling me my womb chakra was blocked. Naturally, I googled "how to clear a blocked sacral chakra" and found ample suggestions.

Once a day, I listened to a chakra clearing meditation with my Carnelian stone tucked into the elastic waistband of my leggings, secured right over my womb. I bought an orange shirt—because the internet told me to surround myself with the color orange—but it wasn't as flattering as I'd imagined, so it hung in my closet with the tags on and

I would occasionally rub the fabric between my fingers, hoping that would do something. I added dancing to my morning routine, with emphasis on hip movement, and prayed that DeAndre would not walk in on my one-woman Zumba class. I went on a shopping spree at the art supplies store and immersed myself in creative pastimes like painting and collage. *A blocked sacral chakra? No ma'am. Not on my watch.*

I stayed deeply committed to my spiritual practice for two months while trying to get pregnant. Then one morning in early September, I stood in the bathroom holding the familiar white plastic stick between my fingers. I stared at the tiny rectangular window as the first pink line appeared, and then, a faint second line.

beginnings

I held the pregnancy test under the bright bathroom light, then by the window to see it in natural light. The second pink line was so light, I wondered if I was hallucinating it. I reached for my phone and focused the camera on the small, rectangular window. I took a photo and examined that, too, in every light level I had at my disposal, before sending it to my group chat.

I asked: *Am I imagining this?*

My friends confirmed: *I see it! It's positive!*

I hadn't felt this exhilarated since I got my first positive pregnancy test in our Brooklyn bathroom after months of obsessively trying to conceive. Since then, every positive test was stained with painful memories and sharp reminders that this gift could be taken away. Pregnancies are supposed to end in beginnings—piercing cries and warm drool on soft lips that remind you a new life has been created with your body—but in two years, we'd only ever known endings.

* * *

We heard the baby's heartbeat at our six-week ultrasound appointment two weeks later, tiptoeing past the first major milestone with a deep sigh of relief. At home, I was fortunately distracted by a laundry list of agonizing pregnancy symptoms, which I lovingly embraced, even though it meant existing on a diet of flavored seltzer water and toasted white bread slathered in butter.

Dr. Goldstein wanted to see us for weekly ultrasound appointments through the eighth week of pregnancy. Having reassurance every seven days that the pregnancy was progressing was supposed to soothe any lingering anxiety—and it did, to an extent—but it also meant I was teetering on the edge of panic once a week.

When we arrived for our seven-week ultrasound, my hands were clammy, and every nerve in my body was vibrating. We heard the heartbeat again, and the gentle melody of soft hooves galloping through the airwaves rocked my trembling nerves to sleep. Hearing our baby's heartbeat gave me a high like nothing I'd ever experienced —carrying this being inside my body and giving shelter to their beating heart was beyond magic. The euphoria lasted for nearly an entire week, only coming down as I anticipated the next appointment.

My anxiety exacerbated my pregnancy symptoms—heightened nausea, low appetite, and physical discomfort irked me as my stomach twisted into tighter knots the closer we were to our next ultrasound. Eight week ultrasounds of pregnancies past were rife with vivid, aching memories—long stretches of silence followed by gentle apologies and an endless stream of tears. I coached myself mentally in the days leading up to that appointment. I made empty promises in an attempt to soothe my anxiety in the moment, telling myself that if all was well at eight weeks, I could rest my weary heart and stop worrying.

* * *

As soon as I found out I was pregnant, I started a list in the notes app on my phone to track all the names I loved. DeAndre and I would often hear a name in passing or on TV and turn to each other to debate if we liked it. Girl names were easier than boy names, but even so, there were few that we agreed on.

"Paloma. I like that name," DeAndre said to me one evening. I think he heard it on TV, or maybe saw it written somewhere.

"Paloma," I said. I always repeated name suggestions out loud. I needed to feel the letters and syllables dance off my tongue before committing it to the list. "Yeah, I really like that!"

The name that sat firmly at the top of my list was Luz. The shape and sound of the word itself was stunning to me, but it was also deeply meaningful. In Spanish, Luz means "light." I could not think of a more fitting name to bestow upon our child, their presence in my belly like glistening gold thread woven around the edges of a passing rain cloud.

I added Paloma to the list and, staying true to form, I googled the meaning behind the name.

Paloma is a female given name, derived from Latin "palumbus," which means "dove."

My mouth fell open slightly as I stared at my screen. I whispered to myself, "Oh. My. God." Dove. Kira's great grandmother. I closed my eyes and said a silent prayer. *Thank you, thank you, thank you.*

* * *

I crossed my arms, my shoulders tense and my jaw tight on the way to our eight-week appointment. We found out we'd lost our first pregnancy at our eight-week ultrasound, and the memory made this milestone that much heavier. Hard as I tried, I couldn't imagine any other reality because I'd never lived it.

We were stopped in early morning rush hour traffic on Venice Boulevard. I looked out the window to my right and saw a green awning over a small storefront—*La Paloma Market*. I dropped my arms and relaxed, allowing myself to be cradled by another message, a warm embrace from above.

* * *

"Your blood pressure is a bit high," the nurse said. "Is everything okay?"

"Yeah. Well, no, actually. I'm really nervous," I said.

"Oh, okay. We'll check your blood pressure again before you leave," she said.

I undressed and sat upright on the exam table. My chest rose and fell as I took deep, controlled breaths. I swung my legs in short motions, bumping the side of the table with the heels of my feet. I deliberately wore socks with a black and white heart pattern on them, deciding last-minute that these socks would be assigned the role of my personal good luck charm. Dr. Goldstein knocked lightly before coming into the room.

"How are you guys doing?" she asked.

I laughed at the audacity of this question. "Terrified, honestly."

"Yeah, that's understandable, after everything you've been through!" she said.

Lying back on the table, I glanced at the ultrasound monitor quickly before looking up at the ceiling. I steadied my gaze on the fluorescent lights above me. Dr. Goldstein was quiet for a few seconds that stretched an eternity.

"There's the baby," she said under her breath as she clicked around the keyboard.

My body tensed in the way that you brace for impact when you are sure you are about to get into a car crash. I prepared myself to be wrecked, almost expected it because it was all I'd ever known. Dr. Goldstein was staring at the monitor. I wanted to yell and ask her what's taking so long. I wanted her to say something, anything to fill the unbearable silence. It hadn't been more than a minute since she started the ultrasound, but a minute of silence was too long.

I gripped the vinyl padded exam table, digging my sweaty fingers into it to stop my hands from shaking. I thought about reaching for DeAndre's hand, but I worried I would squeeze it so hard that I'd fracture all five of his fingers. Then, just as I was about to resign all hope, we heard it—our little drummer serenading us with the sound of their mighty, beating heart.

The heavy sobs rolled out of me like a flash flood. The nurse appeared taken aback as she handed me a box of tissues.

My voice shook, but I assured her, "I'm just so happy!"

On the way out, the nurse checked my blood pressure again, and it was back within a healthy range—proof that my body was continuing to respond to intense memories of past trauma. I wanted to hold my body and promise her that we are safe, give her permission to release the trauma, to shed it like snakeskin, but this was easier said than done.

* * *

In mid-October, we had our nine-week appointment with a regular OBGYN after graduating out of Dr. Goldstein's care in the Reproductive Endocrinology department. Going to a new office with new doctors came with a fresh set of concerns. Dr. Goldstein felt like family, and it rattled me to have to start a relationship with a new doctor. Did they know how fragile I was? Did they know that I needed to be treated with kid-gloves?

The doctor walked into the exam room like a fumbling, chaotic friend out of a 90s sitcom. She fussed loudly with the ultrasound machine, complaining about new equipment that she wasn't familiar with. I could hardly focus on my usual state of panic because the doctor's energy was like a barrage of pots and pans falling from the top shelf. As she continued to fuss with the equipment, I shared a brief history of our miscarriages and how we'd never come this far in any past pregnancies. This was my subtle way of asking her to please fucking chill out before I unwittingly match her chaotic energy and spiral into an emotional meltdown. My concerns were met with grace, and she turned her commotion down a few notches.

As we listened to the heartbeat, she smiled and said, "I think this is the one that's going to make it."

"I think so too."

* * *

The weekly ultrasounds I was getting due to my history, which made me a high-risk patient, stopped after nine weeks, and we had to wait three weeks until our next appointment.

At 11 weeks, I had a standard first-trimester blood test screening to look for any chromosomal concerns. We asked the genetic counselor not to tell us the baby's sex. DeAndre and I had discussed this at length and agreed that we wanted to be surprised in the delivery room.

A few days after the blood draw, I was stopped at a gas station when my phone buzzed. I had a new message from the genetic counselor. I remembered how she told me that she would call if something were concerning. Otherwise, I'd get an email. Before I read it, I was already bouncing in my seat, grinning ear-to-ear. Her message explained that the first-trimester screening results came back normal. I wanted to honk my horn a bunch of times, throw myself a party at the gas pump. I held my phone against my heart, closed my eyes, and rested my head on the headrest. The lingering burden of past pregnancy traumas lifted like a veil. *This is really happening,* I thought. *I'm going to have this baby.*

* * *

I opened my browser that night and pulled up a page I had bookmarked for maternity jeans. I'd dreamed of this day, buying maternity jeans without biting all my nails off, wondering if I'd somehow jinxed myself. I remembered that I still had the *Destination Maternity* gift card that my mom sent me during my first pregnancy. I went to their website and bookmarked potential baby shower dresses. I didn't need maternity clothes yet, but I was eager to get to that phase—willing my belly to grow, yearning for it to become bigger, rounder, full of life.

Babies born after miscarriage are often referred to as "rainbow babies," likening them to the beauty that occurs when the sun shines after a rainstorm. It wasn't my style to drape our baby entirely in rainbow merchandise, but I had seen a few choice pieces of clothing that lit my heart up. I pulled up a link for a T-shirt that I'd been eyeing for more than a year. It had a rainbow printed on the chest, and "Mama" written on top of the rainbow. The vague suggestion of one day being able to wear this made my chest flutter. I put one in my shopping cart, then clicked over to the children's clothing section. There was a matching toddler-sized T-shirt with the same graphic, but "Babe" was written over the rainbow. I added it to my cart and placed my order.

I couldn't wait for the day I would put on my "Rainbow Mama" shirt and walk into the world with it stretched over my round, growing belly. In a few years, I'd pull the "Rainbow Babe" shirt over our child's head and delight strangers with our matching outfits, the colorful screenprints telling a story of stormy endings followed by sunny beginnings.

* * *

Our next ultrasound was in early November. At 12 weeks pregnant, this was another major milestone appointment. They'd take lots of measurements and look for certain risks to the fetus. During the weeks leading up to this day, I envisioned seeing our baby wiggle around on the monitor, their arms and legs visible to us for the first time. My vivid daydreams played out with so much clarity that I choked up every time I got lost in thought, wandering through a fantasy that would soon be our reality.

I wore my new maternity jeans and a purple peplum T-shirt that I hoped made me look pregnant. I rolled down the soft fabric to expose my belly as I lay flat on the exam table. The sonographer briefly explained that she would take measurements first and let us spend time admiring our baby on the screen after. A nurse was standing behind her, assisting. The sonographer turned the monitor toward us so we could watch. She squeezed a glob of warm gel on my stomach, pressed the ultrasound probe into my low belly, and dragged it slowly across my skin.

I couldn't bring myself to look at the image on the screen yet. I looked at DeAndre, who was staring at the monitor. A moment later, the sonographer gently rotated the monitor away from our view without saying a word. The nurse mumbled something I couldn't understand and left the room.

My limbs were frozen, my body ice-cold and sweaty all at once. I couldn't move, but I strained my eyes toward the monitor. I saw the vertical white line travel across the screen, left to right. Then once more. No jagged line appeared behind it. There was no sign of a heartbeat.

endings

The sonographer was so convincing, I almost believed her when she told us, "I think it might be too early in the pregnancy." She uttered those words with the same casual enthusiasm that one might say, "I think I'll have a salad for lunch." She then told us, in the same nonchalant manner, that she was going to find the doctor.

Now alone in the exam room, DeAndre and I remained hauntingly still as we tried to connect the dots. Perhaps the sonographer should have won an Oscar for her performance because I knew she was lying to us, but for those first few minutes—after she turned the monitor away from our view—I chose to believe her. I denied what I knew in my bones to be true as I stared at the ceiling and begged for a better outcome, my mind a tornado ripping apart every happy moment that brought us to this point. My heart pounded in my ears as the minutes passed, so many minutes of silence, waiting for the doctor. I tiptoed around the conversation, finally piercing the silence with a shaky voice.

"This can't be good," I whispered. I looked at DeAndre, hoping he'd say something to make it all better, praying he'd find the words that would carry us somewhere safe and far away from imminent doom.

Our eyes locked for a few slow seconds, as if we were communicating without words. His face dripped with a knowing, perhaps mirroring the story my eyes were telling. We disconnected our gaze—I stared up at the ceiling while DeAndre looked toward the door.

The storm inside my mind calmed, and only a single thought remained, a quiet voice whispering in my ear. I repeated the words out loud.

"It's over." My voice cracked. I stopped fighting and let my tears fall, rolling currents streaming down my face. "I don't want to be alive anymore."

"What did you say?" DeAndre asked. He appeared shaken as he leaned closer to me.

I put my hands over my face and cried. Death felt like my only escape from this recurring nightmare. I never imagined this amount of suffering was even possible for the human spirit to carry. I was sure that the crushing weight of sorrow was going to kill me right there in that room, and I would have welcomed it.

Nearly an hour had gone by before the doctor finally came into the small, gray room. I was lying down still, my body stone on the exam table. DeAndre was sitting next to me, holding my cold, sweaty hand. The doctor squirted a glob of warm gel on my belly and pressed the ultrasound probe into my stomach. I fixed my eyes on her face, but her expression gave nothing away. She looked at the screen for only a few seconds before she swiveled to face us.

"I'm unable to find a heartbeat," she said.

Another ending. Another death in my womb, this shelter where miracles come to die. The humiliation was debilitating—everyone knowing except for us, likely discussing our fate on the other side of the door. How could I have walked into this room with my guard down, a huge smile beaming across my face? What an absolute fucking fool.

"I'll leave you two alone to discuss what you want to do next," the doctor said. As the door clicked shut behind her, I relaxed every muscle I'd been tightening to stop myself from crying in front of her. My tears rained down without mercy.

Our collective pain collapsed into my chest, a mountain of dusty bricks constricting my airways. My soul cracked, fragments drifted away like snowflakes being carried away by a winter breeze. I traveled somewhere outside of my body where I could breathe, where I could look at a different view than the fluorescent lights above. Those lights—why did I stare at them for so long? They will become triggers, reminding me of this moment every time I rest my head on an exam table.

I reached for the small white towel that the sonographer had secured in the waist of my pants an hour ago, and wiped the gel off my skin. I pulled my shirt down and sat up. "I guess I should schedule a D&C," I said. I wiped diluted black mascara from under my eyes with a tissue.

"It's completely your call, whatever you want to do," DeAndre said.

"I can't do this at home. In the toilet?! No," I said, angry and offended at the very idea as if it was presented to me by someone other than my own imagination.

I stood up and reached for the door handle, then stopped myself. DeAndre had watched me cry, held my ice-cold fingers, and listened to me wish death upon myself for the past hour while he remained calm and composed. I hadn't checked in with him once. I took my hand off the door handle and turned to him.

"How are you feeling right now? Do you need anything from me?" I asked.

"I'm okay," he said. His protective armor was on, and I envied him.

We stepped out of the exam room and turned the corner into the nurse's station. My fury billowed when I saw the sonographer and the doctor chatting quietly. They stopped talking and turned to face us as we stepped closer. I tried to appear unemotional, hoping to hide my hostility over how they handled this, how they lied to us and left us alone in that room, wondering if our baby was dead or alive—but even with all their purported missteps, my miscarriage wasn't their fault.

I sat in a chair in the nurse's cubicle while the doctor looked on the computer for an available time to schedule my D&C. The sonographer was standing next to me, and I could feel her ogling me with pity like I was a wounded animal on the side of the road and not a grown woman in pain. She reached her hand to my face, stroking it softly with the backs of her fingers. My face remained unmoved, but I couldn't stop myself from crying. I sat still as tears dripped down my pink, puffy cheeks.

She continued to brush her fingers against my face, and I heard a whimper, an "aww, sweetie" escape her lips. I imagined my skin as broken glass, my body made up of razor-sharp edges poorly pieced together—and I wanted her to cut her finger on me. I wanted to swat her hand away like a housefly, to wrap my fingers firmly around her wrist while I stare at her through bloodshot eyes and tell her to fuck off. We were not in the exam room anymore, and she did not have my permission to touch me. I jerked my face away from her hand, and she pulled back.

"We have availability this afternoon," the doctor said, her eyes scanning the computer screen. "Or you can come back at 10 a.m. tomorrow, but you'll see a different medical team." She turned to look at me.

"Tomorrow," I said, without taking a beat to think it over. I needed a clean slate, to emotionally detach and create as much distance as possible between myself and the people I had been, however unfairly, raging at in my head all morning.

My resentment poured out into the waiting room, full of women with big bellies and couples nudging strollers back and forth in short, steady strokes. We would have to walk through there soon, a forest where the fog smells of sweet baby powder, and soft coos from the cave-like shadows of bassinet strollers pierce my eardrums. I wondered if I could make it all the way to the exit while gazing at my feet. Or perhaps I would keep my head up and allow everyone to see my face, raw and red, force them to hear me wail in anguish—hoping to disturb their peace—because it wasn't fair that they got to have babies, and we didn't.

I hid behind my long, brunette curls as we took the elevator downstairs to the pharmacy to wait for my prescriptions. As we were sitting in the waiting area, my phone rang. I recognized the number and answered.

"Mary, I just heard the news. I'm so sorry," Dr. Goldstein said.

I stood out of my seat and walked briskly out of the pharmacy in search of some semblance of privacy. I paced back and forth in front of the automatic sliding doors. The white, windowed doors opened and closed repeatedly as I held my hand over my face and heaved beneath the sensors. I squatted low to the ground, trying to make myself small. I pressed my back against the building's cold exterior and hid below eye level as the pharmacy's heavy foot traffic picked up with the nearing lunch hour.

"I don't understand what happened. What do we do now? Are we just supposed to keep trying? Keep going through this?" I asked, begging her for the answers that I knew she couldn't give me.

"Oh, Mary, I am so, so sorry," she said. Her voice shook, on the verge of tears. "We'll run all the tests again. We'll talk about your options. Just call me when you're ready, okay?"

I hung up and immediately messaged the genetic counselor who had ordered the first-trimester screening the week prior. I couldn't bear it—I had to twist the knife. I wanted to know everything about the child I was grieving.

I wrote: *Hi, we discovered at our scan today that there was no heartbeat. If you know the sex of the baby, could you please let me know? Thank you.*

She responded within minutes: *Oh, I am so sorry to hear that. The sex chromosomes were normal (XX), which meant the baby was a girl.*

With the message still open, I let go of my phone and watched it fall from my fingers into DeAndre's lap like it was a piece of hot coal. I folded my body over, and with my face pressed into my hands, I erupted into tears in the middle of the crowded pharmacy.

* * *

I believe my intuition—that sudden flash of heat I felt in my belly while the doctor offered options from her calendar—guided me to that 10 a.m. appointment the next day, and when we arrived, I understood why. The nurse spoke to me with such tenderness as she led me down the hall. She delicately honored my unspoken boundaries as she quietly measured my vital signs and then led me into the exam room where she handed me a thick, folded white paper sheet.

I slid off my shoes and tucked them in the corner. I removed my pants and underwear, folded them, and placed them on a chair. I used my arms to hoist myself onto the table, but I was weak—both the valium and hydrocodone they'd given me that morning were beginning to take effect.

The doctor knocked softly before entering the room. She was a young, petite blonde woman with a familiar face and a natural smile that put me at ease. She introduced me to her colleague, a dark-haired man who followed her into the room. He seemed like a kind, charming man—the type of person who regularly goes out of his way to be friendly to the baristas at Starbucks. The doctors told me that they would be assisting each other with the procedure. This pleased me because their presence alone offered a sense of security, allowing my shoulders to drop, my jaw to soften, my legs to hang over the side of the table like soggy noodles.

As I sat on the edge of the exam table, watching them line up metal tools for the procedure, I curled my shoulders forward and wept. Both doctors stopped what they were doing and looked at me. They didn't ogle me like a wounded animal, though. Without either of them saying a word, and perhaps unintentionally, they made it known that their presence was a safe space to fall apart—so I did, and even in their silence they responded with such deep, heartfelt compassion that it radiated my bones. *These must be my guardian angels in lab coats.*

Before the doctor began dilating me, she informed me that she needed to do one last ultrasound. In my increasingly sedated state, I nodded. With heavy eyelids, I looked over her shoulder at the monitor. I saw my daughter's lifeless body suspended in a sea of darkness—she was floating face down like someone had carelessly thrown her body into the ocean, and even I, her own mother, could not save her. The doctor turned her head toward me and caught me staring at the screen. Her shoulders dropped, and her eyelids lowered. My baggage felt lighter, as though she'd taken some of my sadness, lessening the burden on my heart, if only for a brief moment.

A few minutes into the procedure, I heard a baby fussing loudly. The high-pitched sounds traveled from the hallway, through the walls, under the crack beneath the door, and into my ears. I shifted my position slightly and felt the wet, sterile paper sheet underneath me. Loud voices were fawning over the baby now. Their joy was shaking the walls around me. I wondered why there wasn't a separate wing for women like me—trapped in that exam room, hearing sounds of motherhood from my private, anonymous hell. *I wonder if that will ever be me*, I thought. The cramps in my abdomen worsened, sharply reminding me that it's not my time.

After it was over, I took my feet out of the stirrups and slowly sat up. I slid off the table and crumpled the white paper sheet into a big ball before stuffing it into the garbage can. The paper that I was lying on top of had soaked up a pool of blood. I looked down, and there were bright red drops on the gray speckled vinyl floor under the exam table.

of Miscarriage and Motherhood

XXXXX

On the drive home, I leaned my head against the passenger seat headrest and closed my eyes. I couldn't get the image of that final ultrasound out of my mind. She was painted on the backs of my eyelids, her shape chiseled into my brain.

"I saw her on the ultrasound screen. She looked like a baby, she had tiny arms and…" The words made me cry, so I stopped. DeAndre reached over and rested his hand on my thigh, his comforting touch never far from me.

* * *

I crawled into bed with all the necessities: my phone, laptop, painkillers, gummy bears, and chocolate. I turned *The Office* on Netflix—my favorite distraction—and let it run in the background while I drifted in and out of sleep.

I scrolled through the photo album on my phone and found an illustration I'd done right after miscarriage number four: "Do whatever the fuck you need to survive" was drawn in thick, jagged letters over a violet background. Seeing that piece and remembering its origins triggered my rage. I posted it on Instagram again, this time with a long, boiling rant about life being so unkind to us.

Before I logged off for the day, I unfollowed nearly every pregnant person in my feed. I'd pressed the follow button on many pregnant women that summer, strangers I'd admired only through screens, imagining I'd be joining their club any week now as I prepared to announce our miracle and start posting my own occasional pregnancy updates. Now, seeing their baby bump photos appear in my feed knocked the wind out of me.

I sat up in bed, opened my laptop and searched the internet for local Reiki healers. I don't know why this idea entered my mind—I'd never seen a Reiki healer before—but I allowed myself to open up to the invitation to see where it would lead me. I came across April, a Reiki healer in Santa Monica, and I felt my intuition light up like a matchstick. She was the one I wanted to see. I booked an appointment for the following week.

DeAndre checked on me often. He made sure my water cup was always full and that I had enough to eat. He'd lie down next to me and share moments of quiet affection, his body curved against mine, the perimeters of our shapes nestled together like perfect puzzle pieces. I could hear him playing video games in the next room sometimes. The incessant smashing of small plastic buttons under his thumbs, and jarring, howling laughter as he shouted at the game offered solace—a remembering of normalcy, a promise that we will climb our way out of grief once more. I curled up on the couch next to him in the evenings, and we'd eat takeout and watch reality TV.

That weekend, I opened our mailbox to find a thick, pillowy package—the rainbow shirts had arrived. I threw the unopened package in a drawer and cursed at myself, a moment of self-loathing for daring to believe that this pregnancy would be any different. I sealed two pairs of unopened, unworn maternity jeans in a plastic mailer. I wrote "I had a miscarriage" under the *Reason for Return* section on the return slip. Writing those words knowing that a stranger might read them—might feel a tiny slice of my agony as their eyes move across my confession—made my sorrow feel momentarily weightless.

* * *

Aside from booking the Reiki appointment, I had entirely abandoned my spiritual practice, and I was taking poor care of myself. Basic hygiene was a struggle—I only had enough energy to brush my teeth every morning, no motivation to take a shower, and washing my hair was out of the question. I forced myself to drink water, but only enough to balance the wine that I'd start drinking in the late afternoon. Every minute that I was awake, merely existing, was excruciating.

Darkness closed in on me the longer I stayed in bed feeling sorry for myself—eating mouthfuls of gummy bears and chocolate (a delectable combination), greasy takeout, and hydrocodone every six hours. It took five days for me to grow tired of rolling around in my uncomfortable misery, with oily knotted hair and worsening body odor that finally pushed me to take a long, steamy shower.

In an effort to purge my pain, to halt it before it destroyed me from the inside out, I committed to feeling everything. I had lengthy crying sessions where I clutched my pillow and pressed my face into it so I could scream until my throat burned. I pulled out every thread of strength I could find, and I scribbled my rage, tearing holes in the pages of my journal before throwing it to the ground.

Every day, I inched a bit further from despair. Some moments still crashed into me like tidal waves, when I'd see a toddler seated in the front of a shopping cart, helping her mother pick the perfect green pear at the grocery store. I'd begin to cry beneath my sunglasses, abandon my shopping list, and keep my head down until I could get to my car and explode, sobbing until I was gasping for air as I banged my fists on the steering wheel.

Other days were lighter—I'd catch myself laughing at something on the TV, an unfamiliar rush. I could listen to a Beyoncé ballad, which I'd put on for the sole purpose of provoking more tears, and not break down. On a few mornings, I'd drive to the beach, take my shoes off, and trek through the cool, velvety sand. When I met the ocean's edge, I'd stand still and let the ice-cold tide roll over my feet. I'd turn my music up until my earphones were vibrating, close my eyes, and feel chilly November ocean air sting my wet cheeks.

*   *   *

A week after finding out we lost the baby, I had my appointment with April, the Reiki healer. I arrived early for the session and sat in my car for a few minutes. I opened my phone camera and looked at my face. The late afternoon sun was illuminating my skin. Even with the pleasant golden hour light, I looked worn—my skin creased and washed-out, my eyes bloodshot.

April greeted me through the screen door and welcomed me into her space. I took my shoes off, put my bag down by the door, and then followed her into the back room. I lifted myself onto the treatment table and sat up straight with my legs dangling over the side. April stood in front of me, holding a thin silver chain with a pointed crystal pendulum hanging from one end. She tapped the pendulum lightly to put it in motion and moved it upward, holding it for a few seconds in front of each of my chakras. The pendulum stayed in motion, twirling in a perfect circle, only slowing slightly in front of my womb. As she raised it to my heart, it nearly stopped moving.

"You have some heart stuff going on?" she asked softly. Her voice was so soothing, like a crackling fireplace on a chilly evening.

"I had a miscarriage last week. I'm heartbroken," I said. My shoulders sank, and I lowered my head. A few large teardrops fell into my lap.

As I lay on my back under a thick, cream-colored woven blanket, April placed crystals on my body—over each of my chakras—and in both my hands. I curled my fingers around the heavy, smooth stones. She rested a soft mask over my eyes that smelled like fresh lavender. As she began the healing, she stood at the head of the table and spoke softly, just above a whisper, calling in spiritual support for me. She placed her hands on me lightly, cradling my head, shoulders, and arms, moving down my body every few minutes. Sometimes she spoke, repeating mantras, and her silky voice allowed me to drift further into deep rest. When the session was over, I opened my eyes to an air of peace I hadn't felt in months.

Before I left, April twirled the pendulum over my chakras again. As the pendulum stayed steady in motion, I saw that my heart was open. More importantly, I felt it —the bleak, inky stains of hopelessness scrubbed off my heart, if only for today.

I got into my car, pulled the visor flap down, and looked at my face in the mirror. The hard lines on my forehead had softened, and my rosy color was restored.

I was beginning to accept that my dream of motherhood was deferred indefinitely. I was nowhere near ready to try again, and I knew it would be at least several

months before I would get there. Since marrying
DeAndre, I thought I knew what my life would look like:
weekly *Mommy and Me* classes with a room full of
toddlers climbing their mother's bodies like a playground;
afternoons lying in the grass and searching for animals in
the clouds, assigning each one an imaginative name and
personality while they wrap their small hands around a
silver pouch, sipping Capri Sun through a narrow, yellow
straw; and sopping wet high-fives after swim lessons,
every day a little bit closer to toeing the edge of the pale
blue diving board for the first time and leaping into the
water three feet below, stopping for ice cream on the way
home to reward another milestone of bravery. I believed I
could easily create the life I envisioned in my mind
because I was in control, but control was nothing more
than a comforting illusion.

* * *

A few days later, I reached out to Jacqueline again,
desperate for more healing tips, herbal remedies, anything
she could offer that would nourish my bleeding, broken
heart. She connected me with her friend Michelle, an
intuitive reader and second-generation astrologer who
offered thorough, insightful birth chart readings over the
phone.

"Are you an artist?" Michelle asked.

"I am," I said. "An illustrator—mostly on the side, though."

"Good. Keep going with that. I see it in your chart—you are here to give your creative genius to the world. Your art is your gift to the collective and it will transform lives," she said.

My heart pounded when she said those words, affirming what I had lost sight of since I was a child—being an artist is a gift. Full stop.

My pen raced across my notepad as Michelle looked over my chart and continued to speak.

"You're not taking care of yourself," Michelle said. I almost laughed, thinking about how many of my meals in the past few weeks were built around bags of gummy bears and bottles of wine.

"No, I'm not," I said.

I'd struggled to take good care of myself for most of my life—stuck in binge-and-restrict diet cycles and obsessions with exercise solely to achieve thinness, when what my body needed was nourishment. Michelle helped me understand why this was my biggest obstacle in life. She explained that my difficulty taking care of myself was a core wound. This piece of me would take more than kale smoothies and yoga classes to heal—a relief to hear because I'd absolutely tried to remedy this problem in the past with green smoothies and Pilates DVDs, to no avail.

"You're very empathic," she continued. "You're highly sensitive to energy. When something happens, you feel it in your whole body. And you might often feel other people's energy too. Does that resonate?"

I was already nodding. "Oh my god, yes," I said.

"You need to start putting boundaries around your energy," she said.

For a long time, I thought my extremely sensitive nature was a character flaw. I'd feel everything around me so deep in my core that it was debilitating. So often, I would instinctively pick up toxic energetic garbage thrown around by others, whether intentional or not, carrying around their emotional baggage as if it were my own, and not knowing how to dispose of it.

Michelle gave me a detailed prescription for the months ahead. "For the next two weeks, release your pain. Release negativity. The next new moon is going to be big for you—energy is lifting and you're going to feel it. Now, this next piece is important: sacred self-care. What can you do that nourishes your whole self?" she asked. "Sacred self-care is self-care for your mind, body, and spirit. All three. We call it sacred self-care because *you* are sacred. Commit to this for the next year. Be there for yourself first so you can be there for your family. I guarantee that this journey into yourself will be the best thing you have ever done. Mary, you are going to need to be vigilant about your healing. You will have your heart's desires met.

You *will* be a mother, okay? You *are* a mother. You have to turn those maternal instincts on yourself."

sacred circles

Jacqueline invited me to go hiking with her on a Sunday afternoon in early December. I had turned down all social invitations the past few weeks, canceled dinner plans, even left some texts unanswered. By December, I was finally ready to come out of bereavement hibernation—and spending time in nature was part of my sacred self-care agenda—so it was an easy yes to her invitation.

My legs turned to jelly almost immediately as we climbed up the steep trail. I hadn't moved my body much, other than casual long walks when I was pregnant, in months. My face dripped with sweat as I tried to keep up with Jacqueline, who said she wanted to jog to the top. I waved her away and stepped off the trail to catch my breath. More groups of people passed me by while I leaned over, breathing heavily as I stared at the ground, wondering if I might decorate it with my vomit.

Jacqueline was waiting at the top of the trail, smiling and cheering for me as I stumbled toward her 20 minutes later. We planted ourselves in the dirt at the edge of the canyon and took in the view of Malibu Beach below—the sapphire horizon glistening under a clear sky. We sipped cold nettle tea that Jacqueline had made and brought in her canteen. My heart pounded and my body trembled, but this time not from emotional distress or anxiety, and not inside an exam room. For the first time in weeks, I felt entirely present in my body. The sun on my skin, drying the slick layer of salty sweat, and blood rolling through my veins—a well-timed reminder that I was still alive.

On our way back down the trail, I steered the conversation toward the only topic on my mind these days: healing. Jacqueline happily indulged me. I told her about my birth chart reading with Michelle and my new sacred self-care syllabus. I shared all the ideas Michelle laid out for me: guided meditations, moon rituals, aromatherapy with flower essences, dietary changes, more Reiki healing.

"Have you ever tried breathwork?" Jacqueline asked.

"No, what's that?" I asked, already prepared to agree to whatever she was about to suggest.

"During breathwork, you lie flat on your back and breathe a specific way, like quick deep breaths into your belly and chest, and it's all through the mouth. My friend Madeline is holding a breath circle this Thursday," she said. She stopped in her tracks and turned to me. "You know what? You're coming with me."

"Okay!" I said, skipping a few steps and kicking up a small dust cloud in my excitement.

"You're going to love it. Last time I went to a breathwork circle, everyone ended up hysterically crying and screaming together on the floor."

I laughed, expecting her to say she was kidding, but the punchline never came.

* * *

Heartfelt Dreams with Mother Mary was the theme of the breath circle that Thursday night. When I walked in, I saw Madeline sitting on the floor at the front of the large room, lit with candles and orange salt lamps glowing in every corner. Her long, blonde, wavy hair fell over her shoulders, and she wore a floor-length white dress with loose, flowy sleeves.

Large glass jars of warm, rose tulsi tea sat on either side of Madeline. She set out a stack of small cups and encouraged everyone to help themselves. In front of her was the altar she'd created for the evening. A small Mother Mary statue stood in the center, surrounded by white candles, red roses, and selenite crystal wands. She'd fanned out oracle cards in a circle around the display.

Jacqueline was sitting on a mat, chatting with a small group of people—never shy, she'd always made friends so easily. I unrolled my mat next to hers and sat down. As I scanned the room, looking at each of the 15 or so strangers around me, I wondered if I belonged here.

I hadn't felt this insecure since fifth grade, when my family moved from Orange, California to Aurora, Colorado right in the middle of the school year. I arrived in the second semester, trying to fit in with my Midwestern peers but doing a terrible job because sunny Southern California fashion just didn't translate to the snowy 'burbs of Colorado. My brand new chunky black hiking boots and abstract patterned fleece pullover did not have my new classmates flocking to welcome me into their friend groups. I walked into homeroom on my first day beaming with confidence, certain that I would be embraced by the cool kids because at my old school, I was one of them. At my new school, they ignored me, and for the rest of the school year, I remained somewhat of a loner, an outsider.

We sat in a circle around the altar, and Madeline led us in a short opening prayer as we held hands. She directed us to each choose an oracle card. I crawled to the center of the circle, picked a random card, and turned it over as I scooted back to my seat. It had a painting of the ocean on it. I didn't know how to interpret it, how to connect to it. I stared at the card longer, at the paint strokes coming together to form a vast turquoise ocean against a sunset sky. *I love living near the ocean*, I thought. *Am I doing this right?*

Taking turns to receive the group's full attention, each person around the circle shared their oracle card and a few words, and some shared their personal intention for the evening. My heart started beating faster as my turn approached. As I spoke, my voice shook, attempting to remember the speech I had nervously prepared in my head for the last five minutes.

"I pulled this card. It has the ocean on it," I said, holding up the card. "I moved back to California from New York last year because I love living near the beach, so this makes sense." I heard myself babble on, and I sounded ridiculous. My cheeks were hot and probably bright red, the dim orange glow of the room thankfully disguising my embarrassment. I took a deep breath. "I'm here tonight because a month ago, I had a miscarriage. It was my fifth in less than two years." My voice began to crack, and I heard a soft chorus of sympathetic murmurs from one side of the circle. "I'm just trying to heal." I sobbed into my hands.

I could feel all eyes on me—everyone in the room was witnessing my heartbreak. Unlike the humiliation of falling apart in the pharmacy or on an exam table, where those around me often winced in discomfort or looked at me with pity, this group held space for my sorrow. Without a hint of judgment, they just looked me in my eyes and listened.

We spread out around the room on individual mats, lying under cozy blankets brought from home, our eyes covered with soft sleep masks. Some people brought crystals or other small tokens that they placed at the head of their mats. I made a mental note of this for next time.

Madeline turned on music and guided us into the breath healing. "In through the mouth, into the low belly, up into the chest, out through the mouth." She set the pace with her voice, three quick breaths repeating in sequence. "Inhale, inhale, exhale."

The music got louder, drowning out the chaos in my mind—the constant burden of an overthinker. The steady rhythm of everyone's breath overlapped like soft instruments blending with the music. A few people in the room let out loud sobs. Their willingness to let go of restraint, plus the music muffling the sound of our voices, was freeing. Hearing their emotional release gave me permission to unhook my latch. My gate swung open with force, and my sorrow flooded out with a wailing sound.

When we're young children, we cry as loud as our feelings demand, no matter where we are or who is around. As adults, rarely do we give ourselves that freedom. Screaming, gut-wrenching crying sessions were reserved for lonely moments in my bedroom, preferably with my face in a pillow. Here in this room, I allowed myself to literally cry like a baby.

Under my blanket, my body was cold. My fingers awkwardly curled and froze as they rested by my side, which Madeline explained might happen from energy moving and releasing from the heart space out through the hands. She told us not to worry, that if this happened, it would naturally resolve.

"You don't have to carry this alone. Hand it over to Mother Mary," Madeline said as she walked around the room. Aretha Franklin singing "Let It Be" blared through the speakers, and I bawled harder. Madeline telling us to hand it over to Mother Mary as Aretha sang "in my hour of darkness, she is standing right in front of me" sent a surge of adrenaline through my body. It was as if all the heavy burdens weighing my heart down were suddenly tangible—massive, decaying entities. I tore through each one, destroying them with my breath, a machete made of air.

At one point, Madeline placed her hands on my ankles, then squeezed my feet lightly. She dabbed oil on my forehead and chest with her fingertips, and I inhaled aromas of floral and citrus.

After about 30 minutes of breathing, the music faded to a low volume.

"Start to slow down your breathing. You may want to wiggle your fingers and toes. Take your time coming back into the room," Madeline said.

I took off my eye cover, which was damp from crying, and rubbed my eyes with the palms of my hands. My body was tingling, and I felt like I was suspended in space, floating above the earth. I put one hand on the floor to confirm it was still there. My mind buzzed, intoxicated by what I'd just experienced.

After Madeline closed out the evening with a prayer, we rolled up our mats and gathered our belongings. On my way out, I introduced myself to her and told her I couldn't wait to attend more of her breath circles.

* * *

Ten days later, I drove to a holistic healing space in Long Beach to attend my first new moon circle. Brook—a friend of both Jacqueline and Michelle—held these ceremonies on every new moon. I still didn't quite understand what I was getting into when I signed up, but Michelle told me that this new moon—landing on my 35th birthday—was going to be potent for me. In my vigilant quest for healing, I secured my spot the moment Michelle sent me the link after our reading.

I stepped lightly through a sliding door into a large room with wood floors. I chose a space near the corner to put my bag down and roll out my yoga mat. I sat down, pulled out my journal and pen, and a small purple velvet pouch with a few of my favorite crystals.

Tapestries hung on the walls. The lights were low, the whole room a soft amber color. In the center of the room was a striped burgundy blanket beneath the altar—an arrangement of crystals, fresh roses, and candles. People kept shuffling into the room, the space becoming tighter as we all scooted closer together to make room for everyone attending the sold out ceremony.

"If you brought anything to charge on the altar, go ahead and add them," Brook said as she stood at the front of the room. She was barefoot, wearing a loose white dress with colorful embroidery around the neckline. Her straight, sandy blonde hair hung over one shoulder.

People on both sides of me crawled forward and placed items on the altar—Tarot decks, books, candles, crystals. I timidly placed my pouch on the outer edge of the blanket, pretending like this was totally normal to me even though I felt like I was a visitor on a faraway planet trying to learn rituals of another species. Madeline's breath circle was a warmup for Brook's ceremony, where I was so far out of my comfort zone that I almost grabbed my belongings and snuck out before the ceremony began.

Everyone around me was chatting with one another and it was clear that most of them were regulars. I sat in my corner with my shoulders back and chin up, doing my best to soften my expression and appear approachable so that I might make a friend for the evening.

Brook walked around the circle and greeted everyone individually. She wafted resin smoke over each of us, waving a feather to fan the smoke around each person and energetically cleanse the circle. The aroma gave notes of a roaring campfire under a night sky, the nostalgia of sitting shoulder-to-shoulder with my best friends on a Girl Scout camping trip.

When Brook completed her introductions around the room, she sat crossed-legged on the floor at the head of the circle. She described the significance of the new moon —the beginning of a lunar cycle. New moons are a powerful time to set intentions, create or renew goals, and manifest desires, as the new moon symbolizes a new beginning.

Brook handed out tall white candles in clear glass holders. The ritual that evening—which was different every new moon—was to craft vision spell candles. Per instructions sent in advance to the attendees, we brought images and words cut out of magazines or, in my case, hand drawn and then cut out of my sketchbook.

I decorated my candle with images that represented everything happening in my life and what I desired—a butterfly to symbolize transformation, angel wings for spiritual support, a rose, the words "nourishment" and "create," a figure holding her heart, a healthy womb.

I went home that evening and placed my vision spell candle on my nightstand. I lit the candle, its orange flame swaying as I sat in bed and wrote in my journal:

I miss my daughter. I would have been 18 weeks pregnant today. It hurts. But I try not to think about it. It's over and gone. I hope she will come back to us one day soon. I am on a different journey now. I am trying so hard. Thank you for what I have learned by having you and losing you. I know I will be a better person and mother for having gone through it. But I miss you so much.

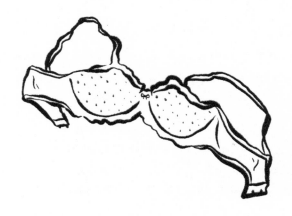

discoveries

Every morning was the same. I'd wake up in an empty bed and remember, like a swift kick to the gut, that I was alone in my body. Two months after losing the baby, I still endured this startling realization those first few seconds after opening my eyes. Sometimes I dreamed I was still pregnant, and I'd lie in bed a few minutes longer, debating if I should even bother putting my feet on the floor. Measuring my heartache became second nature, part of my new daily routine as morning light seeped through the blinds, and I lay in bed, rubbing the sleep from my eyes. Eventually, I'd sit up, toss the covers off me, and stand to stretch.

I studied my body in the long mirror that hung on our closet door. Though I'd never developed a baby bump, my body was puffy from pregnancy hormones. As my hormones settled after the miscarriage, I admired the changes—my jawline was sharper, my waist more curved. My body was returning to its old familiar shape, and I found solace within its borders, as if I could pretend that her life had not existed here, and that she did not die inside me. My eyes traveled the length of my curves, and I made silent vows to shower my skin in love, to forgive myself, and to release any blame for life lost inside my womb.

It was a Monday morning in January, exactly two months since she was taken from us. My bare feet touched the cold hardwood floor, and I sat on the edge of the bed for a moment. I stood up and reached my arms overhead, raising myself onto the balls of my feet for the kind of full-body stretch that is so intoxicating, it makes you catch yourself on the wall to keep from falling over. I crossed my forearms in front of me and gripped the bottom seam of my shirt with both hands. As I pulled my shirt overhead slowly, I looked at my reflection in the mirror. Bare belly and breasts, everything soft and elongated—I consumed my reflection like it was a work of art.

Something caught my eye at this angle, a tiny protrusion on the underside of my left breast. I turned my body at different angles to get a full view of my discovery. I compared it to my right breast, thinking maybe this was a characteristic I'd never noticed in my breasts. It was only on the left side, though. I rubbed my fingers over it. I poked it, and it didn't move. It was hard, more firm than cartilage but not quite bone.

I changed into a red sweatshirt, clean underwear, and leggings—comfort over everything since I was now working entirely from home after the office space lease ended at my startup job and my boss decided not to renew. After I brushed my teeth, I came back to the closet mirror. I lifted my shirt and examined my breast again, hoping I'd find nothing this time, hoping I'd imagined the bump, but it was still there.

I went into the kitchen and pulled two mugs from the cupboard. I scooped three heaps of ground coffee into a French press and topped it with boiling hot water from a kettle. I set a timer for four minutes and leaned against the kitchen counter. I watched ribbons of steam hover above the French press while I slid my hand beneath my shirt and grazed my fingertip along the crease under my left breast, rubbing lightly back and forth over the smooth, round bump.

I set DeAndre's coffee on his desk, where he'd been for at least an hour before my alarm woke me up, and sat down at my desk. I had every intention of working, but found myself staring at a flashing cursor in the internet search bar. Everyone says not to google these things. Easier said than done, though—that empty search bar is dreadfully enticing—and down the rabbit hole I went.

I discreetly reached my hand under my shirt to examine the bump again. I poked it repeatedly as I compared it to the results on my screen. Does it move? Is it hard? Is the skin puckered? My internet searches lured me toward some dark holes, but I focused my attention on the results that showed anything but cancer. *It's probably a cyst or something,* I thought, not the least bit convinced by my benign suggestion. The bump and the area around it were tender to the touch because of my constant, aggressive poking. I closed my internet browser and refused to give the little bump any more attention.

* * *

I opened my eyes as my alarm chimed at 7 a.m. and immediately reached my fingers under my shirt. The bump hurt when I touched it, like a ripe bruise. I got out of bed and looked at it closely in the mirror—it was unchanged.

I sighed heavily. "Fuck," I said, accepting the frustrating realization that I was going to have to deal with this.

I drafted a text to Gretchen: *I found a lump.*

I deleted it and retyped it: *What should I do if I found a lump in my breast?*

I didn't want to send it, to say any of this out loud. I wished I could go back to childhood, to a time when my mom made all my doctor's appointments. She'd pick me up halfway through the school day—leaving early was a treat I looked forward to all morning—and take me for a checkup, then out for a soft serve ice cream cone.

Gretchen and I continued to text back and forth. She asked me to describe the texture, the hardness, the density, the mobility of my lump. I scrutinized every characteristic again. I took pictures and sent them to her —a small crescent moon shadow under my breast, a tiny dimple puckering my skin.

I logged onto my doctor's office online portal to make an appointment, anything to avoid telling a stranger over the phone, "I found a lump in my breast." My throat tightened at the mere thought of saying those words out loud. I clicked through the calendar online, but there was nothing available for weeks. The knots in my stomach were multiplying and I could feel the color drain from my face. DeAndre was sitting at his desk perpendicular to mine and turned to look at me as I rested my elbows on my desk, my jaw heavy in the palms of my hands.

"What's wrong?" he asked.

I opened my mouth, but tears trickled out ahead of my words. "I found a lump in my breast," I said. I cried harder and covered my face with my hands. "I'm really scared."

"Oh, babe, I'm sorry. Everything is going to be okay. Let's go to the doctor. I'm sure it's nothing," he said. He locked his eyes with mine and didn't look away until I nodded in agreement.

I patted my face dry and reluctantly called the appointment line. I asked to see anyone anywhere for the first available opening. They offered me an appointment the following afternoon at a new location, a little farther than the facility we'd been going to for ultrasounds during my pregnancy.

* * *

We arrived at 2 p.m., and I paced up and down the hallway—lined with benches where other patients sat and waited—until a nurse called my name almost a half-hour later.

Seated on the exam table, I held my gown closed with both hands as we waited for the doctor. DeAndre sat in the corner, neither of us interested in cutting the silence with small talk. When the doctor came in, I slid the gown from my shoulders and leaned back. I raised my left arm over my head and pointed to the lump with my right hand. She examined my left breast, then my right breast. Not even five minutes later, I was dressed and walking out of the facility with a referral and phone number to the radiology department.

I dialed the number from the parking lot, but the receptionist told me there was nothing available for 10 days. The thought of waiting 10 whole days made my head spin. I accepted the first available appointment, went home, and prayed for an earlier opening.

The next morning, I called the radiology department again as soon as I woke up, sitting up in bed with my legs still cozy under the covers. I quietly yawned as the receptionist searched for an opening. There had been a cancellation, and she offered me an appointment for the following day at 7:30 a.m. I hung up and whispered a dozen thank yous to my empty bedroom.

* * *

In the radiology department, I was welcomed by a sign that read *Women's Area* on the door. A nurse handed me a gown and a clear plastic handle bag, instructing me to change into the gown and put my shirt and bra in the bag.

The pale blue dotted gown hung well past my knees. I took a seat in the waiting room, the plastic bag cradled in my lap, and looked around. Scenic nature murals covered two walls. Bright green leaves and glossy blue skies contrasted with the drab, sterile waiting room.

Everyone in this waiting area appeared significantly older than me. They made small talk with each other, exchanging sighs and sharing woes of the dreaded annual mammogram. I pretended not to notice that the other women did a double-take when I walked in. I tucked my chin down, hiding my face in shame as if I'd done something wrong to end up there, as if I had any reason to shrink in my seat from embarrassment.

During the ultrasound, I cranked my neck to see the monitor while the sonographer pressed the probe into my breast. I examined her face, trying to read her expression, but she didn't flinch. I turned my head toward the ceiling and saw the familiar fluorescent lights—hard edges and glaring hues still haunting me months later.

After the ultrasound, the doctor came in and told me that I'd be getting a mammogram. Sitting in the cold plastic chair as that word sank in—a word I shouldn't have had to fear for another 10 years—I am reminded of one particular day when I was 13-years-old and standing in my friend's living room. Her mom swung her purse over her shoulder, headed toward the door, and told us, in all seriousness, "Alright, I'm going to my annual boob smashing appointment. See you girls later." As I was about to learn, that is a remarkably accurate description.

My lump sat so deep in my breast that I wondered if it was welded to my ribcage. This meant a lot of pulling, yanking my breasts like silly putty, and contorting my body around the huge machine—with all its rigid, unfriendly surfaces—to get a clear picture of it. The mammographer apologized and joked that these machines were designed for people without heads. I laughed, a moment of levity as the machine clamped down hard on my breast.

"I'm going to go show these to the doctor," the mammographer said, waving a manila folder.

I sat in the corner of the room with my gown loosely draped over my shoulders and pink stickers stuck to my nipples.

The doctor came into the room a minute later. "Hi, Ms. Purdie? I looked over your mammogram results, and I want to do a biopsy," he said. "Come with me, and we'll get that scheduled."

I peeled the stickers off my breasts and pulled my shirt back on. The doctor escorted me to a nurse to make the appointment. She was cheery and talkative as she opened the calendar on her computer. I could only see her mouth moving, though. The sound of her voice was drowned out by my pulse, pounding like a bass drum in my ears. Alarm bells in my mind rang, and the surge of panic rushing through my body threatened my balance. I leaned against the wall while the nurse stared at the calendar on her screen.

The earliest available appointment for the biopsy was more than a week away. More waiting. I didn't have it in me to push or negotiate. I was ready to go home and manage my anxiety in private—soothe my inner chaos with a hot bath and a mellow playlist. I entered the appointment in my phone's calendar and stood to leave. On my way out, the doctor passed me in the hall.

"Did you get an appointment?" he asked.

"Yes, January 22nd," I said.

"That's the first available? Hmm, wait here." He walked away and turned the corner into the nurse's station. Not even a minute later, he came back around the corner and directed me toward the nurse. "Something opened up on Monday. She'll get that moved for you," he said with a smile so big it unnerved me.

* * *

For the next few days, I suppressed everything inside me to appear at ease—a feat that proved unsuccessful. I drifted in and out of crying spells without warning—in the shower, over the stove while I cooked dinner, in front of the TV watching bad reality shows.

We didn't speak of the terrorizing thoughts that were likely dominating both our minds, but DeAndre was so tender that weekend as if we had an unspoken understanding. He showed me grace, squeezing my hand as we sat next to each other on the couch, offering to get takeout from a restaurant of my choosing, and putting a moratorium on our usual sarcastic banter—a pillar of our relationship, a daily love language built on playfully roasting each other.

Miscarriage felt so small compared to this. Losing our babies was just awful, but what if we lose me? I pressed my palms together every morning and began bargaining.

Please let me live a long life, even if it's only to be with DeAndre. I won't ask for anything else, but please give me this.

* * *

As the days passed, I buried myself in art, my faithful companion. I processed the myriad of feelings—striking me in such quick succession it felt like emotional channel-surfing inside my brain and body—through illustrating them in the most simplified way. A cardboard box labeled "FRAGILE - PLEASE HANDLE WITH CARE" sat against a pale pink background. White feathers falling into a pile at the bottom of the page with the word "Soften" written in rounded, intertwining letters. A yellow and white spiral layered under a question, drawn with shaky black lines, that I'd read in a book borrowed from a friend: "What is this trying to teach me?"

About a month earlier, I received a direct message on Instagram from a young man. He shared with me that his mother was battling advanced-stage cancer. He thanked me for my art—which by that time had become a public expression of my deepest vulnerabilities and little else—and said it was helping him cope. We exchanged a few messages that day. I didn't hear from him again until the evening after my biopsy. He shared that his mother had just passed away, and he thanked me again for being a source of comfort through social media.

I was in the kitchen cutting vegetables when his message came through. I read it, then put my phone on the kitchen counter next to the cutting board. I picked up the knife and kept cutting. As the blade sliced through raw sweet potato, giant teardrops fell onto the counter. I heaved, sobbing louder as I processed his message, overwhelmed with sadness as I thought about the burden that cancer leaves behind for families and friends to carry. I wondered if this was preparing me.

* * *

My phone rang around 11:20 a.m. on January 17th, just two days after my biopsy. I was at my desk looking up bed and breakfasts on my computer. I had been holding on to a gift card that my parents gave us more than a year ago with the sentiment that after all we had been through, three miscarriages at that point, we deserved a weekend away. I was saving it for a babymoon, perhaps a weekend in Santa Barbara or Palm Springs, walking along the beach or sitting poolside with a giant baby bump in tow. That wasn't my reality anymore, though, so it was time to book the damn getaway. DeAndre was sitting at his desk in front of me on a conference call with his colleagues. My heart thumped and my breath became shallow as I answered my phone.

"Hi, Ms. Purdie. I have the results from your biopsy. Unfortunately, we did find cancer," the doctor said.

I listened, nodding along and clenching my jaw, tightening every muscle in my face to create a wall that tears could not penetrate—not yet. He kept talking, explaining that the cancer was treatable, and going over the next steps we would take. I relaxed my face and sobbed into the phone as the conversation ended.

DeAndre looked over at me and abruptly interrupted his meeting. "I have to go. I'm sorry, I have to get off the phone right now," he said. He yanked his earphones out with one hand and jumped out of his seat. His chair slid across the hardwood floor, almost tipping over from the momentum of his movement.

"I have breast cancer!" I yelled.

DeAndre walked around my desk and reached out his hand. "Come here," he said. I stood from my seat and buried my wet face in his chest. He wrapped both arms tightly around me as I heaved. "We are going to beat this," he said in a low, gentle tone. He rubbed his hands across my upper back and repeated those words before squeezing me tighter, pulling me closer to his chest, the safest place in the world.

"We're going to beat this, right?" I asked, muffled, my face pressed into the thick fabric of his sweatshirt.

"Yes, babe. We are," he said.

perspective

I considered waiting another day to tell my mom and sister that I was just diagnosed with breast cancer, all too aware of the role I had taken on as the poster girl for depressing news. I texted them separately a few hours after I got the call, asking them to call me at their convenience. The last thing I wanted was for them to step out of a meeting at work or be standing on a busy street when I said the words that would shake the ground beneath their feet.

Gretchen texted me back with urgency: *Should I call right now???*

I replied: *No, you can wait until you get home.*

A few years ago, I was sitting on the subway on my way to work when I received a text alerting me that a friend had passed away. I read the message just as I stepped off the train into heavy commuter traffic. I gasped for air as I walked up the stairs out of the station. When I made it outside, I leaned against the nearest building with my hands on my knees. I stared at the sidewalk and sobbed—my breath a delicate, white cloud in the ice-cold winter air—as morning commuters passed by in droves. This memory was fresh in my mind, and it was why I refused to tell my sister "I have cancer" until she was safe and sound at home.

I delivered the news to my mom and Gretchen separately. "The doctor called. I have breast cancer," I said, my voice firm in an attempt to sound brave. My words were met with outbursts, bellowing thunder preceding a sudden storm. My tears joined theirs, and our collective despair moved like thick, gray clouds, stretching from California, over my parents' home in Colorado, and all the way to New York.

* * *

Though we didn't work together anymore, Alyssa and I kept in touch on social media and I saw that she was holding a virtual new moon ceremony that evening. After Brook's ceremony the month before, this ritual— honoring the beginning of a new lunar cycle—sparked a small fire inside me, a place to warm my hands as I wandered down the dark, desolate halls of grief. The sense of community within these ceremonies highlighted human connection, each of us links on a chain, perhaps reaching for a common goal: spiritual enlightenment, healing old and new wounds, waking up to our higher purpose.

My eyes were rubbed raw when I logged into Zoom for Alyssa's ceremony that evening. I lit a candle on my nightstand and sat in bed with my laptop perched on a pillow in front of me. When it was my turn to speak, I put both hands on my heart and said, "I was diagnosed with breast cancer this morning." I was barely able to get the words out before I collapsed into tears.

There were only five women on the call, and I saw each of their eyes widen and their mouths fall open as I confessed my devastating diagnosis. Maybe that's all I needed to make it real to me—to be witnessed by others as I said the words out loud, unraveling by candlelight alone in my bedroom.

* * *

I had emailed Michelle earlier that day, a casual SOS:

> *Hi Michelle, I hope you're well! So, life has taken a turn. I found out today that I have breast cancer. I was just wondering if you could recommend any healing modalities for me right now, perhaps specific to healing cancer?*

The news hadn't yet sunk in as I typed my message, evident by my nonchalant tone, relaying my major life update as if I was telling her I had a paper cut and needed suggestions for the best topical ointment.

After the ceremony, I checked my email and found an urgent reply from Michelle: *Can you talk now??*

I answered her phone call with an awkward laugh, all cried out from the moon ceremony and still teetering in disbelief over my new reality.

"I'm so sorry you're dealing with this," Michelle said. "I know this is hard to believe right now, but you are going to be okay. You're going to be okay. I promise." She repeated those words over and over during our call, potent affirmations I held in the palm of my hand until I began to believe them. *I am going to be okay.* Michelle continued, "I know you will come out of this experience more powerful. It feels impossible, but just trust, okay?"

"I'm trying," I said. My heart was numb as I listened, plucking choice words from Michelle's speech to remind myself later.

"Be brave, Mary. I really want you to open yourself up to where this journey takes you. These experiences can offer so many gifts if we stay open to them. Start asking your pain and grief, 'What am I supposed to learn from this? What is this showing me?' Allow yourself to receive nurturing as you continue to process your grief. Hold your breasts, give them love, talk to them," she said.

I was nodding along with tears in my eyes. Michelle was reminding me to love my sick body, going against every impulse I had to curse and demonize it. I felt my edges soften as I sat in bed with my phone in my hand.

At the end of our conversation, Michelle said with tenderness in her voice, "You've made a soul contract to be a healer. Sometimes these things happen when a healer needs to be reminded of their gifts."

This idea—though not brand new to me since I'd been consuming all kinds of spiritual literature lately—that this could be happening to teach me something, to awaken me, was frustrating at first. I did not want to do another heavy course load of Spiritual Awakening 101. I wanted to have an epic meltdown and tear through my belongings like a rabid animal. I wanted to throw heavy objects against the wall and scream expletives until my vocal cords were blistered and raw. I was fucking exhausted, and I'd had enough. But, to my surprise, Michelle's words didn't fan my flames—they snuffed out my five-alarm fire, as if her words were the antidote to my deepest fears.

I had spent the better part of the past two years vacillating between different levels of anger and self-pity over everything I'd had to endure, and it only proved to wear me down. I dreamed of breathing fire in the face of anyone who dared to say to me, "Everything happens for a reason," because I do believe that is a bullshit platitude and should never ever be uttered in place of sympathy. When one comes to that conclusion on their own, though, if only to give us a minuscule dose of hope when all else fails, it can be powerfully healing. With my cancer diagnosis slowly sinking in, I was ready to put down my weapons of rage and pivot to a new perspective.

* * *

The next evening, I invited two friends to come with me to Madeline's breath circle. I unrolled my mat in the far corner of the dimly lit room and pulled my small velvet pouch from my bag. I unwrapped a heavy quartz crystal point and placed it at the head of my mat.

My heart pounded as we gathered in a circle, my friends on either side of me. I listened as others shared what was on their hearts—relationship conflicts, work troubles, journeys of self-love. The mood was light, there were no tears yet, and I was struck with a pang of guilt.

"Yesterday, I was diagnosed with breast cancer," I said. My voice shook, but I kept going. "I want to believe that this is happening for a reason and it will make sense one day. Maybe this is teaching me something. I don't know. It's scary right now, but I know I will get through this." I rested my hands on my knees while tears poured from my eyes and hung on my jaw like early morning dew drops on a windowsill. There was a long moment where no one spoke, and I closed my eyes and cried while friends and strangers patiently looked on.

I wrapped myself in a blanket on my mat as Madeline started the music. My friends were lying on either side of me, their presence a life raft keeping me afloat. A few minutes into the breathing, "I'll Stand By You" by The Pretenders came on. Those first few notes roared through the room, and I deepened my breath. "When the night falls on you, you don't know what to do…" The lyrics rushed through my veins like sweet medicine, and I wailed loudly, rain and thunder escaping my lips. For the next several months, I'd listen to this song over and over, as if it were required to keep me alive. I'd play it loudly while I sat in the bath with the lights off, candles lit, and a piece of rose quartz resting on my chest. Chrissie Hynde's voice cocooned me as my tears fell into the warm bathwater in a steady stream.

* * *

DeAndre accompanied me to my first appointment with the breast cancer surgeon that Friday afternoon. The nurse who brought us into the exam room was talkative— perhaps on auto-pilot—as she offered unsolicited speeches about life and death.

"You'll get through this, don't worry," she said. "I've seen many friends overcome this. After all, no one is promised tomorrow. We could walk outside and get hit by a bus today."

DeAndre and I nodded and smiled as she spoke. My body tensed, unsettled as I listened to her ramble on about our odds of getting killed in a freak accident as if these hypotheticals would dilute my very real cancer diagnosis. I wanted to politely hold up my hand, ask her to stop before my mind spiraled into a blackout so deep that I would not be able to return to the present moment.

The surgeon came in with a stack of papers, my diagnosis highlighted in yellow on top:

Stage 1A 95% hormone-positive, HER-2 negative invasive ductal carcinoma

She went over my treatment plan, which was still partially unknown. She explained that my tumor was so small, I'd only require a lumpectomy to remove it. Then they'd test it further and determine if I'd need more aggressive treatment like chemotherapy. She confirmed that I would be getting radiation, followed by long-term medication in the form of a daily pill to block the hormones that caused the cancer to grow.

She paused to ask if I had any questions. My words escaped as if I had no control, powerless to pull them back in.

"When can I get pregnant again?" I asked.

She frowned, then took a deep breath. "You have to be on this medication for at least five years, and you can't get pregnant while you're taking it," she said.

Five years. The words punched me. We had come *so far* trying to have a child, and though in my desperation I'd promised to never ask for this again, I didn't want to bargain that dream away.

When she left the room a few minutes later, DeAndre turned to face me. "Mary, I don't give a fuck about that, okay? You need to get better. That's all I care about," he said. He appeared distraught. His eyes held mine as if he was looking past them, trying to read my thoughts.

I know that he was in the right mindset, but I couldn't meet him there. I couldn't remove the desire from my mind, even temporarily. Giving myself this—a commitment to have children one day—was keeping me above water. Running toward a future I'd always imagined, or at least some version of it, was another reason to stay alive. At the same time, DeAndre was scared of losing his wife. The thought of dying was scary, but having to keep living after the love of your life dies? I couldn't fathom a worse fate.

"Okay," I said. "You're right. I need to get better."

An hour and a half into this appointment, we were sitting in a cancer coordinator's office, a title I didn't know existed. She handed me pamphlets, one by one, for local cancer support groups and wig services. Seeing wig catalogs disoriented me. The pile of papers in my lap grew heavy, and I wanted to give them all back. I wanted to stand up and let the papers fall to the floor, run down the hall and out the door and keep running until sweat poured through every inch of my clothing and my legs gave out beneath me.

The nurse led us back into the exam room a few minutes later. I sat on the exam table with my hands wrapped around the stack of pamphlets and catalogs, each one shouting CANCER PATIENT in big, bold letters. My new reality slapped me across the face, my skin burning with a red hot handprint as the words sunk in. *It's me. I'm the cancer patient.* I stared at the vinyl flooring as the cliffs of my eyes held puddles, blurring my vision until they spilled over the edges, warm streams gliding down my cheeks. The nurse looked at me as I quickly tried to wipe away my tears. She seemed surprised, pausing mid-sentence before rushing from behind her computer to console me. She cradled my hand in hers.

"Disease doesn't have to mean death. You never know who you will help by going through this yourself," she said.

I nodded, wiping my nose with a tissue in my free hand.

I was despondent in the passenger seat of our car after the appointment.

"Let's go to the movies," DeAndre said. He grabbed my hand and drove us to the nearest mall, a field trip to balance out the traumatic events of the day.

We stopped for lunch near the theater, and as I sat down with a salad and mint lemonade, my phone rang.

"Mary, your surgeon just called me," Dr. Goldstein said. She paused, and I imagined her frozen at her desk in shock.

"Hi Dr. Goldstein. So, can you believe this?" I asked. I laughed—the only thing I could do to stop myself from falling to pieces inside Tender Greens.

"I just wanted to say that you should consider freezing your eggs. I'll send you fertility clinic referrals, and we can talk about your options," she said. Her suggestion made my urgency feel justified, validating my choice to ask all the absurd questions still swirling through my brain.

* * *

For a few weeks, I didn't share the news with anyone outside of my close circle. I wanted to shout it, beg everyone around me—friends and internet strangers alike —to pour love into me. I illustrated words Michelle said to me on the day of my diagnosis—in pale pink and cobalt blue, it read, "Trust. Be Brave. It's going to be okay." Then, a pair of red boxing gloves hanging against a blue-gray background. The words "You will find your strength" curved around the strings. I grieved as loud as I could, in the vaguest way possible.

Two weeks after being diagnosed, I received an email:

> *Hello! I'm sure you get requests all the time, but I am a cancer survivor walking in New York Fashion Week on February 11th, and at the after-party, the designer is auctioning off artwork where all the proceeds go to breast cancer research. Would you be interested in donating anything?*

My mouth fell open. I wrote back and shared my recent diagnosis, emphasizing my utter disbelief at the timing of her email, and offered to donate three pieces of art.

I dismissed this as an incredible coincidence until a few days later, when a company contacted me requesting to collaborate on a small series of social media posts illustrating uplifting phrases. On the conference call to discuss the project, they said, "We'd love to have the first post done by February 4th for World Cancer Day."

Perhaps that was the pivotal moment when I stopped believing in coincidences because these were not random events. These were clear messages, gentle hands pressing on my back, nudging me forward. I took a step and listened closely. I heard my inner voice telling me, "*This* is your path! Run this way, and do not be afraid!"

dreams

"Mary, I need you here. That's it. Nothing else matters to me," DeAndre said. He was sitting on one end of the couch, facing forward. I was on the other end, studying his profile as he spoke. Holding eye contact during these conversations was rare.

I need you here. His tone was dripping, heavy and slow like honey but without the sweetness. I momentarily drifted to that dark place where I'd spent a lot of time in recent weeks before shaking myself out of it.

"But... I'm not going anywhere," I said. My lower lip quivered, an inevitable side effect anytime the slightest indication of death crossed our lips. *I need you here.*

"Sorry, I didn't mean it like that. I just need you to realize that *I only need you*," he said.

We'd attempted this discussion morning, noon, and night for an entire week about whether or not to preserve my fertility, but we still hadn't agreed on a solution. One of us always got frustrated, and we had to walk away, spare ourselves the stress of an argument. Unfortunately, time was no longer a luxury we could afford. My surgery was fast approaching, and treatment would start soon after. We didn't have months to weigh the pros and cons —we had to decide to go through with freezing my eggs or risk losing the option to have biological children.

I asked DeAndre if he'd meet with a fertility specialist, and he shrugged in agreement, however reluctant. I made an urgent appointment for a consultation at the fertility clinic Dr. Goldstein recommended.

* * *

We sat across from the doctor at the fertility clinic as she meticulously explained everything we needed to know about my fertility and the preservation process. I'd have to give myself injections in my abdomen every day and come to the clinic for ultrasounds and bloodwork every other morning. In less than two weeks, I'd be ready for my egg retrieval.

Since I was a cancer patient, the clinic approved me to receive free medication provided by two different organizations: Livestrong Foundation and Walgreens' Heartbeat Program. The clinic also offered us a 40% discount. This brought the price from nearly $14,000 to around $8,000. I backed off, hoping that, if nothing else, the "cancer coupon" would sway DeAndre.

"I guess we should just do it," he said later that day.

The pit in my stomach dissolved, the jagged, rocky edges softening into warm, silky sand.

We returned a few days later to meet with a nurse and learn how to inject the medications. We decided to freeze embryos instead of eggs because they explained that we'd have more immediate information about how many potentially viable embryos we'd have to use in the future. However, this option came with a caveat.

"You know your relationship better than anyone," the doctor said, looking at me. "But if you decided to split up, you would need DeAndre's permission to use the embryos. If you freeze your eggs, you won't have to worry about that, but the embryos will legally belong to both of you. We will have you sign legal paperwork if you choose to freeze embryos. You will have to decide beforehand what you both agree to do with the embryos in case of divorce or death."

As we walked out of the clinic, I reached for DeAndre's hand and gave it a light tug. "Hey, you better let me keep our embryos if we break up. You won't need them with your ultra strong super-sperm." The bleak morbidity of the doctor's speech faded from our periphery, and we both laughed.

* * *

With all the necessary medication stocked in our refrigerator, I waited for my period so that we could begin the tedious but speedy process. By some lucky fate, the clinic was a 15-minute walk from our apartment in downtown L.A., where we'd moved just after I was diagnosed.

The morning after my period arrived, I woke up with the sun and reluctantly emerged from the warm comfort of my bed. I yawned as I slid on a pair of jeans that were slung over my desk chair and a soft gray cotton T-shirt printed with my own design—a small rainbow pattern, and among the colorful arches it read "Find Joy." I walked to the clinic as the sky burst orange and yellow, over the 110 freeway overpass as rush hour traffic was just beginning. I arrived at the clinic just after 7 a.m. There was only a two-hour window for fertility monitoring, and it was first come, first served. I put my name on the list and waited for the nurse to call me.

The waiting room felt like a secret club. Forest green chairs lined the beige walls. Stacks of old, weathered magazines on every end table, and a coffee maker in one corner. Next to the reception window, there was a sign that read, in bold black type, *Please be sensitive to our patients and do not bring young children to your appointments.*

161

Every evening at 9 p.m., I took out tiny vials of liquid medication from the fridge and filled a syringe. I rubbed an alcohol pad on one side of my stomach—alternating sides every day—and pinched an inch of skin with two fingers. I whimpered the first time I had to poke myself with a needle, but after a few days, it was nothing. Tiny red specks and violet shadows decorated my stomach, and I became increasingly bloated with each injection. Every other morning, I rolled out of bed and walked to the clinic, the crisp morning air jolting me awake. Blood draw, follicle count, and back home with a warm latte in hand from the Starbucks across the street from the clinic.

Toward the middle of the second week, I had to go to the clinic every morning to monitor my ovaries more closely so they could pinpoint the best day for my egg retrieval. By day ten, I had morphed into a human water balloon, worried that buttoning my jeans around my bloated waist would cause me to pop and send my deflated flesh soaring through the air. My follicle count was 13, which meant I had 13 potential eggs ready to be retrieved. The doctor scheduled my egg retrieval for two days later.

* * *

We arrived at the clinic before 7 a.m. and right away they led us into a separate waiting area near the operating room. The nurse gave me a pale gray gown and a sheer, bright blue hair cover. She stuck a thick, black adhesive thermometer strip across my forehead to monitor my temperature. DeAndre sat at my bedside until it was go-time.

An hour later, they were wheeling me into the operating room as DeAndre kissed me goodbye. My vision went blurry and faded to darkness as the anesthesia dripped into my IV. The nurses lifted my thighs to secure them in stirrups, and I went to sleep.

I woke up in a haze in the recovery room, intense cramps twisting inside my abdomen. I turned from side to side in the hospital bed, curling my body and trying to find a comfortable position that would alleviate the cramps. The nurse saw me stirring and told me DeAndre would be coming in soon.

"I'm in pain," I told her.

She brought me two pills and a cup of water.

The doctor came to my bedside, and I blinked my eyes wide open, giving her my full attention in my foggy state.

"Hi Mary. Good news, we got 11 eggs," she said. "Nine of them look great at this stage, and we're going to see if the other two will catch up. The embryologist will monitor all of them and create embryos. We will be watching them for the next few days to determine their quality. I'll see you back in my office in a week to go over the results, okay?"

As the pain in my abdomen subsided, I changed out of the gown and into the pajamas I'd worn to the clinic that morning. I lowered myself into a wheelchair, and the nurse wheeled me downstairs and outside where DeAndre was waiting with the car.

When I met with the doctor the following week, she handed me a photograph of our embryos and a chart with information for each one, not that I understood any of it, but seeing the photos made my heart swell—seven bumpy gray circles, a keepsake bringing me closer to my dreams.

I hung the picture on the refrigerator where I could see them every day. Some days hurt more than others, looking at the images of our embryos and not being able to do anything with them just yet. Like the *Destination Maternity* gift card still sitting in my wallet four years later, and the matching rainbow T-shirts still hiding in the back of my drawer—bittersweet reminders of what was, and hopefully, what will be.

* * *

After the last miscarriage, our doctors encouraged us to explore gestational surrogacy, where another woman would become pregnant with our embryo through IVF and give birth to our baby. Dr. Goldstein said the words with hesitation in her voice, probably knowing that single sentence would break me.

"I recommend at this stage that you consider gestational surrogacy."

DeAndre and I sat across from her as she rested her hands on her dark, wooden desk and awaited our reactions. I sank in my seat, leaning on the armrest closest to DeAndre. I brought my hand to my face and burst into sobs, my shoulders shaking as I created a visor with my hand to shield my face—every trembling curl of my lip, twitch of my brow, and wrinkle in my chin—as I felt my heart break.

Accepting the reality that my body may not be our child's first home, that I may not have the chance to intimately bond with them for those nine months in the womb, was too upsetting to imagine. I may not feel their first kicks or be able to sing to them while I rub my fingers over a growing bump. I may not have stories about which foods I craved while they were growing inside me or which foods I couldn't keep down.

I often fantasize about being pregnant, but I can't linger there too long because even years later, the idea of being pregnant triggers heart-racing anxiety. When I imagine walking into an ultrasound appointment, wondering if I'll hear a heartbeat, I feel faint, and I have to shake myself out of it.

At times, I catch DeAndre grinning, deepening the sharp indents in his cheeks, and I'll say, "I wonder if our children will have your dimples."

On days when I am stubborn and I pick petty fights with DeAndre, he'll say, "If our kids act up, they'll get that from you." These moments sweep away tension, bringing levity as we debate through smiles and butterflies in my belly which traits we'll pass on.

When I sleep late, we talk about a future where infant cries puncture quiet nights and sleeping in will be a distant memory. When I make breakfast on Sunday mornings, I envision an extra plate, brightly colored with grooves for separating food groups. I'd fill the sections with banana slices and fluffy pancakes for small hands to tear apart and dip into an oozing puddle of golden maple syrup.

We can't help but walk through the children's aisle at the shoe store and pick up a tiny sneaker. I hold it up in the palm of my hand and push out my bottom lip because this shoe is the cutest thing I've ever seen, and DeAndre laughs quietly, perhaps picturing himself slipping it on our baby's foot one day.

I think about the moments that stand out from my childhood, praying I may get the chance to recreate a version of those memories with my own children. Perhaps, if they are like me, they will lay their head next to me on Sunday evenings and enjoy the timeless comedic genius of *I Love Lucy* while I sit on the edge of the couch and fold warm laundry. Maybe DeAndre will buy matching helmets for long Saturday bike rides that are rewarded with salty fries, vanilla milkshakes, and stories they will treasure for decades.

Sometimes it feels so far away, the daydreaming slices through my heart like a knife. On those days, all I can say is, "I want a baby," with longing in my voice. DeAndre looks at me and says, without hesitation, "It'll happen."

the sisterhood

I stood in front of the bathroom mirror and pulled my long, curly hair back with both hands. I smoothed the top and sides, tugging it tight against my head, trying to envision what I would look like bald. I dropped my hair immediately, letting it fall over my shoulders. "Nope, I'm not losing my hair. I can't," I said. I turned away from my reflection.

I'd always hated my curly hair as a child, wishing I could trade in my loose ringlets for easy to manage stick-straight hair like many of my friends had. I envied their on-trend 90s bangs, one wispy layer of hair curled under with a three-inch curling iron and glued in place with a half bottle of sticky hairspray. I'd spend hours straightening my hair on Sunday nights—a task I kept up for the better part of my early teens—and still, I always ended up with a few rogue waves that gave me away.

Adults often fawned over my hair color when I was young, telling my mom within earshot of me, "Look at those natural red highlights! She's so lucky!"

I'd roll my eyes at this comment that I'd heard a hundred times before, as if all these people had a pact with each other to trick me into thinking I had the most beautiful red hair when all I saw was boring, brown frizz. When I turned 15, I learned how to bleach my hair at home, thanks to Gretchen and her cool friends, and a few trips to Sally Beauty Supply. The bleach turned my hair orange, of course, which I covered up with my go-to Hot Hot Pink shade of Manic Panic hair dye. Every two weeks, I'd get bored and strip away the color with bleach again before lathering it in a new shade—Violet Night, Wildfire Red, Voodoo Blue. Eventually, my bleaching habit caused my hair to break off near the roots, which isn't as dramatic as it sounds considering I was always up for a big change and loved having my hair short.

My hair was my favorite form of expression during my painfully awkward teenage years. In the summer before eighth grade, my hair hung just past my shoulders and was so obnoxiously thick that I decided to give myself an undercut and shave off all the hair below my temples. A few months into the school year, I started going out with a boy who had the exact same haircut.

I entered high school with a pixie cut, which I gelled within an inch of its life, tugging the ends with my fingers as I held the blow dryer close and on the highest heat setting so my hair stuck straight out all over my head. I clipped my bangs to one side with yellow and red plastic bow barrettes, the kind I wore as a kid. By senior year of high school, I was dying my hair—now a partially grown out pixie cut with short, blunt bangs—jet black every six weeks and straightening it every morning.

When I went off to college, I stopped messing with my hair so much. I let it grow long and, finally, fully embraced my curls. I grew out the black hair dye and, by sophomore year, my natural brunette curls were hanging well past my shoulders. I learned how to properly style my hair with moisturizing curl creams and blow dry it with a diffuser to keep my curls bouncy.

Working at salons in my twenties and thirties only emboldened my obsession with my hair. My stylist friends offered their creative expertise and skills, adding soft ombré highlights and cutting each individual tendril with precision. My hair was my favorite feature, the curtain I hid behind when I felt uncomfortable, my boost of confidence in moments when I couldn't find anything else to love about my appearance. And now, I was fraught with fear—cancer was threatening to take it away.

I made a daily habit of my awkward mirror exercise—pulling my hair tight against my head to examine the shape of my skull from all angles—while waiting to find out if I'd need chemotherapy, all the while remaining happily in denial. My cancer diagnosis was Stage I, and my tumor was only two centimeters—I would not need chemotherapy. No way, not gonna happen.

* * *

In February, I had a lumpectomy to remove the tumor, followed by two more surgeries over the next three weeks because that's how many attempts it took to get clear margins. They told me my tumor was deep. *No shit.*

As I waited for the results, I compared myself to famous people who had been diagnosed with early-stage breast cancer and were now thriving even though they didn't endure chemotherapy—Sheryl Crow, Christina Applegate, Cynthia Nixon. I decided that I would be like them.

I put the wig catalogs in a corner in my closet and refused to touch them. The moment those unsolicited glossy pages landed on my fingertips, I was pulled back into that phone call, retraumatized by the words, "We found cancer." I heard those words every time I caught a glimpse of the thick stack of catalogs and brochures, now tucked away in a plastic hospital to-go bag in the shadows of my closet with all the shoes I never wore anymore.

* * *

On the advice of a friend, I joined a Facebook support group for young survivors of breast cancer. I scrolled through the group posts for hours every day, reading others' stories and updates, and chiming in to commiserate or offer words of support. I often dumped my feelings into the group, describing every worry I was experiencing and asking what others' did when they faced similar crossroads. *Did you freeze your eggs? How many oncologists did you see before you found the right one? How did you decide on your treatment? Did you ever challenge your doctors?*

When that Facebook group was quiet, I searched for other breast cancer support groups and requested to join three more. I had endless content to scroll since most of these groups had hundreds, if not thousands of members. My nervous heart relaxed when I'd read uplifting posts—people celebrating five or 10 years cancer-free, photos of last chemotherapy sessions, or a post-cancer birth announcement, complete with pink newborn cheeks resting against mastectomy scars.

There were other posts that cracked the earth beneath my feet, leaving me frozen in front of my computer and hearing nothing but the sound of my slow breath as heaviness spread throughout my belly.

*Hey sisters, I am sorry to announce that Nadia
passed away last night.*

I clicked on Nadia's profile and tried to piece her life
together through family photos and status updates, get to
know her from a distance, just enough to feel like this was
now my loss too. I'd sit and stare at her picture until I'd
convinced myself I was staring at a friend, and suddenly, I
was overwhelmed with sadness.

It wasn't just Nadia. It seemed like every time I logged
into Facebook, another member of one of these groups
had died. I braced myself every time I opened the app.
When I saw another announcement that someone had
passed away, I clicked on their profile, scrolling until my
heart hurt and tears filled my eyes.

I wanted to distance myself from these spaces the
more I watched people succumb to this insidious disease,
day after day. I couldn't, though—that would be betrayal.
I told myself to stay loyal to the sisterhood, shamed
myself into staying, scrolling, clicking, reading, grieving.

I saw Julia's post at the top of the page when I logged
in one afternoon. She'd posted one sentence: *Just found
out I'm stage 4.*

I scrolled through at least a hundred comments left
underneath, desperate to know more. Julia was 27-years-
old and a few years out of treatment when she found out
her breast cancer had spread.

Four days later, someone in the group who was close with Julia posted an update.

I'm so sorry to tell you all that Julia passed away yesterday. She went to the hospital for a nosebleed that wouldn't stop, and after they admitted her, her health declined quickly. She was surrounded by her family when she passed. If you have any messages for them, I can pass them along.

I tried to understand how this could have happened to her as I read through comments from people who had been in the group for years and knew her, but I couldn't string together the words left underneath—a hurricane of shock, rage, and heartache raining down on me, alone in my room, until I was drenched.

I became consumed by thoughts of death. *What if I'm next? Is it even worth it to fight this? Will I have to carry this fear with me forever?* The more scared I was, the more I devoured posts in the support group until their suffering became my own. I couldn't help but dip my toes into our collective despair, and it quickly overpowered me—a violent riptide pulling me away from shore.

I thought about Julia every night when I went to sleep and again when I woke up. I was in a constant state of mourning over this young woman I didn't know, her Facebook profile picture burned into my brain.

I went into the kitchen early one morning to make breakfast. I grabbed a container of rolled oats from the cupboard and started filling a small pot with water. I peered over the sink into the living room where DeAndre was sitting on the couch. He looked up at me, the corners of his mouth turned down and his eyes vacant. I asked him what he was thinking about and if everything was okay. He hesitated, shaking his head slightly.

"Hey," I said, in a soft voice. "Whatever it is, please tell me." I had a horrible feeling he was about to meet me in the dark place, the emotional dungeon that I had been trying to escape for days.

"I had a really sad dream," he said. He lowered his eyes.

My voice caught in my throat and I started to cry. I knew. I didn't need to confirm it but I did. "Did you dream that I died?" I asked him.

He looked up at me, and our eyes met. Then he nodded.

I dropped the pot in the sink and sobbed into my hands. DeAndre came into the kitchen and hugged me. Everything I'd been holding inside broke free, spilling out of me like an avalanche. I confessed that I couldn't stop thinking about dying. I shared Julia's story, how she was so young and she passed so suddenly. *Was she scared as she lay in her hospital bed? Did anyone gently brush their fingers through her hair and say to her, "It's okay. I'll never leave*

175

your side." Did someone hold her hand and tell her they love her as she took her last breath? How many will mourn her? Who will keep her name on their lips to be sure that she is never forgotten? I threw my head back and screamed through tears.

I told myself that it was time to leave the support groups. I thought about what Michelle told me during my reading in November, that I need to put more boundaries around my energy. My skin was too thin, my heart too fragile to withstand all our pain—a torrential downpour cascading through my newsfeed. I'd hover my cursor over the *Leave Group* button at least once a day, but I didn't allow myself to click it. I was energetically tangled, tied to these strangers, and powerless to sever the cord.

* * *

As I continued to wade in our collective suffering, my mind wandering to death a hundred times a day, I started practicing a simple ritual at bedtime every night. As I folded back the covers and slid my body between the sheets, I'd ask silently, *What do I need to heal? What does my heart need to heal?* I imagined the answer would arrive in a majestic dream. Perhaps I'd wake up with brilliant clarity of mind and the sensation that angels had visited me in my sleep. Three days into this practice, I woke up and reached for my phone. I had a new email from

Madeline, who I hadn't seen since her last breath circle two months ago.

> *Dear Mary,*
>
> *I felt called to reach out and invite you to a Mount Shasta retreat I am leading over Memorial Day, called Heartfelt Dreams. It will focus on deep self-care, nourishment, and attuning to the heart – the sacred center that is connected to the breasts. When I tuned into kindred spirits who would resonate with this retreat and the container it holds, your face popped up :)*

Like magic, my questions had been answered—Madeline's retreat in Mount Shasta was the next step in my healing. I'd known that she was holding this retreat, but I dismissed it when I first heard about it because it would be taking place in the middle of treatment. It was also far away, a 10-hour drive from home. I remember how I lit up the first time Madeline mentioned it at her last breath circle and how my heart sank when I realized it would probably be impossible for me to be there. But it was clear now that this wasn't up for debate—I was supposed to be there, and I would have to figure out how to make it work.

I immediately called Gretchen and told her about my ritual and waking up to Madeline's email.

"I really want to go. I'm just nervous about traveling alone during treatment," I said, dropping heavy hints though not explicitly inviting her because I didn't want her to feel obligated to go as my security blanket.

Gretchen read the retreat details on Madeline's website while I lay in bed with the phone to my ear, quietly listening. "This sounds amazing. I think I want to go, too. I mean, if you don't mind," she said.

I exhaled. "I was hoping you'd say that."

*　*　*

I was alone in the bedroom a few days later when my surgeon called. She told me that she had the pathology results from the tumor, and the cancer scored just high enough on the risk-of-recurrence scale to recommend chemotherapy. My body deflated as I listened to her explain why they would push me to get chemotherapy, how I had many years ahead of me, and how throwing everything at it would give me the best chance of staying cancer-free. I told her I'd think about it and consider all my options. She paused, then gently said, "Mary, please do the chemo."

noise

DeAndre came into the room and found me sitting on the edge of the bed, folded over and in tears.

"They told me I need chemo. I don't want to lose my hair!" I sobbed. DeAndre sat next to me and rubbed his hand across my back, shoulders shaking as I continued to weep.

My plans for skating through treatment without chemo were off the table, though I wasn't entirely convinced, or perhaps I was still clinging to denial. Either way, I was certain I needed a second opinion. I loathed the oncologist they had assigned me. During my second appointment with him, I attempted to have a dialogue about what my treatment might look like and how it will affect our timeline for having children.

"I read that some doctors support taking a break from the medication after a few years to try for a baby..." I began, my voice trailing off because the doctor was already shaking his head.

"No," he said. And that was the end of the discussion. *Okay, Dr. Dick. We're done here.*

I scheduled an appointment with a different oncologist for a second opinion. Then a third, and eventually fourth opinion from an out-of-network oncologist who specialized in integrative medicine. I brought in long lists of questions and recorded the audio of our appointments with my phone. I had only one goal: to hear any one of these doctors tell me they didn't think chemotherapy was necessary.

* * *

The first meeting was with the breast cancer specialist at the facility where I was going to receive treatment. Our question and answer time lasted 38 minutes. She was visibly exhausted at the end of our appointment as I continued to challenge her with monotonous questions. I had moved from asking questions about medicine to philosophical questions like, "Do you think that for some patients, no matter what they do, their cancer will come back if it's meant to come back?" My throat became dry and my voice scratchy as I asked every painstaking question I'd come up with from too many internet deep-dives. The doctor stayed sharp, though, looking me in my eyes while responding to every tedious theory I pitched at her.

The next doctor I saw spent only eight minutes with me, passively nodding and giving me one-word answers to my long list of questions. I was relieved the appointment was short because I knew from the moment he weakly shook my hand that I would not be pursuing a patient-doctor relationship with him.

Between appointments, I read propaganda that claimed conventional cancer treatment would poison me, and researched natural remedies that vaguely promised to eradicate cancer cells—months-long juice fasts, strong herbal teas, and the winner for most bizarre cure: eating whole, frozen lemons.

I put out a call for help from anyone in my network who had been touched by cancer in one way or another. Every time I told a friend about my diagnosis, they shared that they had a family member or a friend, or a friend of a friend's neighbor from high school who had cancer, and offered to connect me. I took every single one of them up on their invitation, building an army of insightful strangers to shed light on the scary, winding path ahead of me. Through connecting with other survivors, though, I got mixed advice, which only clouded my judgment more.

"I didn't do any chemo or radiation, but I completely changed my diet and lifestyle. I have to be perfect about my diet now, though, probably forever," one woman told me. *Ugh, on second thought, chemo sounds more appealing than never eating dairy again.*

"Only you can decide what is best for you, but I think you can heal yourself without chemo. Wake up every morning and say 'thank you' to your immune system. Your body will respond to your thoughts. Nourish yourself with green juice and nutrient-dense meals," another woman told me. *Hmm, tempting. This is more my speed.*

"Listen, I've heard all the 'heal yourself' bullshit advice that people give. You want to know what I think? You don't fuck around with cancer. Do whatever treatment your doctors recommend," another woman said. *Fuck, that stings. I'm listening.*

And finally, the most helpful advice I received through my cancer survivor outreach tour was from a woman who said, "No one can make this decision for you. Everyone is going to have different advice and different beliefs. Block out the noise and choose whichever path brings *you* the most peace."

The decision finally clicked for me when I was talking to my mom on the phone one night.

"I don't want to do chemotherapy. I just really don't even think I need it," I said. "But DeAndre really wants me to go through with it."

"Honey, that's because he's scared of losing you," my mom said, her voice breaking.

I blinked back tears. When I hung up the phone, I stood up and shook my entire body, flailing my arms with loose wrists in front of me and kicking my feet, one at a time, in short bursts out to the side—physically ridding myself of the mishmash of energetic shit I had absorbed through talking to other people.

I came out of the bedroom and stood in the kitchen, my chin up and shoulders back, quietly commanding DeAndre's attention. He was sitting on the couch in the living room, and turned to look up at me.

"Okay," I announced with a sigh. "I'm going to do chemo."

DeAndre nodded. "Good," he said. "I'm glad."

I chose to see the breast cancer specialist—who put up with my 38-minute pop quiz—and go through with the regimen of chemotherapy that every doctor I saw recommended, despite my best efforts to convince them otherwise. I would be getting chemotherapy every three weeks, six rounds total. I emailed my new oncologist in advance and asked her to schedule my chemotherapy around Madeline's Mount Shasta retreat because, as I saw it, that too was part of my treatment.

* * *

During my second-opinion tour, the out-of-network oncologist recommended I start practicing yoga.

I'd always feared yoga studios, full of thin women with flawless skin and chiseled abs. I used to flirt with the idea of joining a yoga studio when I lived in New York City. I would research and read reviews online, sometimes book a free introductory class before canceling at the last minute. I read a review once that claimed a yoga instructor loudly shamed someone in front of the entire class because they were breathing too loud. Yeah, no thanks. If I wanted to be yelled at during my workout, I'd dust off my old Jillian Michaels DVDs.

The doctor was adamant with her suggestion, though. "Do yoga throughout your chemotherapy treatment," she said. "It will do wonders."

I found a studio in my neighborhood and reluctantly sent a terrifying email inviting myself to attend my first ever yoga class that Thursday evening. It was a beginner yoga class, and I'd exchanged a few emails with the instructor in advance to let her know that I was brand new to yoga, so please be patient with my wobbly attempts at downward facing dog, and don't judge me if I surrender halfway through class and fold my body face down on the ground in child's pose.

The studio was on the sixth floor of an old historic office building in downtown L.A., a half-mile walk from our apartment. I'd expected a typical yoga studio—a large, brightly lit space with hardwood floors and wall-to-ceiling mirrors all around the room, also known as my worst nightmare. The space was less like a traditional yoga studio and more like an unfurnished studio apartment. Large windows overlooked the central courtyard of the building. The floor was carpeted, a soft surface for my feet to land as I took off my shoes by the door. I hung my bag on a hook on the wall and unrolled my mat. Crystals, salt lamps, and candles lined the windowsills. The space could comfortably fit eight students, plus the instructor. Between the size and the ambiance, I felt like I was in my own bedroom.

I had unfairly judged yoga. I'd always thought it seemed too slow and low-impact to qualify as actual exercise, the heart-thumping kind that makes your entire body sweaty and so satisfyingly sore that you can feel yourself getting stronger. I could not have been more wrong.

When I walked out of my first class, my body was awakened like it hadn't been in months, maybe years. My posture was straighter, my limbs stronger, my mind undisturbed. Ashlee, the instructor, was everything I'd needed. She was patient, kind, and—my favorite—

generous with rewards. She'd talk softly, instructing subtle movements.

"Mary, turn your left foot out a little more." I'd turn my foot out and hear Ashlee whisper, "Yes!"

Hearing an emphatic "yes!" from Ashlee throughout class fueled me, leaving me glowing with pride as I rolled up my mat an hour later.

After just a few classes, I understood why that doctor told me to begin practicing yoga. Every class was a deep exploration of strength and stillness, improving balance and form, all while savoring an hour of silence within. Even when there were other students in the class, I felt like I was in an intimate meeting with only myself. Ideas for art would flow freely into my mind while I held poses on my mat, and gratitude toward my body began to blossom.

* * *

DeAndre and I arrived for my first chemotherapy appointment on a Tuesday morning in mid-April. I sat in a large, cushioned chair with teal upholstery that looked like a hospital version of a La-Z Boy recliner. The nurse placed the IV in my arm and started my first chemotherapy drip. I watched the clear liquid flow through the tube into my veins. When the bag was empty, the machine beeped until the nurse came over and replaced it with different chemotherapy medicine. I rested my head back as the medicine dripped through my IV. So far, chemotherapy was incredibly boring.

I sat in bed that evening, expecting the side effects to hit me hard and fast like a speeding bus, but I felt relatively normal for the first 24 hours. I booked an infrared sauna session the next day and walked to Whole Foods for a fresh green juice. By the following evening, my body was beginning to ache all over, so I soaked in an Epsom salt bath for a half-hour before snuggling into bed.

The gross, medicinal stench of the chemo drugs seeping through my pores woke me up the next morning. The sour, stale odor worsened my nausea, which was otherwise mild. My body ached like I had been in a minor car accident, everything tight and slightly out of place.

For the next few days, I had to give myself shots in my abdomen to keep my white blood cell count from depleting and protect my immune system. I'd become a pro at sticking myself in the stomach with needles thanks to the egg retrieval process, but the side effects of these injections were much more severe than uncomfortable bloating. I'd read about bone pain, a side effect repeatedly described when people discussed the injections. Painful bones were a foreign concept to me, a sensation I couldn't even imagine, but the way others described this side effect terrified me.

I woke up the next morning and rolled over, every movement of my body sending a crushing sensation through my bones. My hip bones were sore, my legs throbbed in pain, my skull ached. Lying in bed, I massaged my head with my hands. I pulled my knees toward my chest and pressed my fingers into my shins, rubbing in small circular motions. There was no relief to be had—every curve of my skeleton felt bruised.

The bone pain was severe for the next several days, eventually fading and making room for more side effects. The second week of chemo misery delivered a parched mouth and dull taste buds. Water alone made my stomach lurch, so I mixed in apple juice to hydrate myself without gagging. Arrogantly, I thought I would be drinking kale smoothies and cooking nourishing, homemade meals throughout chemo, but I couldn't stomach much of anything. Everything I attempted to eat fell into one of two taste categories: flavorless or metallic. I sent DeAndre out for tuna sandwiches, salty potato chips, and coconut chocolate ice cream bars.

* * *

Every morning before I got out of bed, I'd sit up and look at my pillow. I expected to see a bird's nest, strands of hair that slipped out of my scalp as I slept. I'd tug lightly at the roots to test its strength, but my hair remained firmly planted in my scalp for more than 10 days after my first chemo infusion.

On day 12, DeAndre suggested we go for a walk and see a movie in the neighborhood since my energy was returning. In the shower that morning, I carefully combed through my long hair with a wide-tooth comb while my conditioner set in, my usual routine. Gobs of hair wrapped around the comb. I tugged a small chunk of hair near my scalp, and it slid out of my head with ease. Wide-eyed, I kept combing, pulling the hair off the comb, and putting it in a pile in the corner of the shower. I turned off the shower and called DeAndre into the bathroom. I stood in my towel, touching the hair that was left on my head—surprisingly, a lot—as the wet strands dripped down my shoulders.

"My hair," I said.

DeAndre looked confused as he glanced at the hair on my head.

"I just combed half of it out." I pointed to the pile of hair, a creature nestled in the corner of our shower.

He peeked inside the shower. "Whoa," he said, his mouth agape.

We'd talked about this day, but it stunned me to face it, my final hours before going bald.

When we got home from the movies that evening, I held up a mirror to see the back of my head. My hair was tangled, matted in some areas. Pieces that had slid out of my scalp throughout the day were wrapped around the ends, and I was two twigs away from a bird making a home on my head. DeAndre offered to shave my head the next morning, but I didn't want to wait until then.

"Let's just get it over with," I sighed.

DeAndre set up a chair in the bathroom, sat down, and handed me his clippers. "I'll go first," he said.

He gave me a brief tutorial on how to properly use the clippers, and I nervously shaved his head, pushing the buzzing clippers through his hair as thick, black curls fell to the floor. I rubbed the soft stubble on his round head, laughing with tears in my eyes. It was my turn.

I sat down, wrapped a midnight blue towel around my shoulders, and stared at myself in the mirror. DeAndre cut the long knots out of my hair with scissors until I resembled the Barbie dolls whose hair I used to carelessly chop off at the roots for fun when I was a kid. He took the clippers to my head and buzzed away the rest until I saw G.I. Jane. It shocked me, but I didn't hate it.

DeAndre stared at me for a minute, and I thought he might say something deeply profound.

"What?? Why are you looking at me like that?" I asked, my fingertips grazing the soft stubble on the back of my head.

"I mean... damn. You look hot!" he said with a huge grin.

My cheeks turned pink as I turned back to see my reflection. I smiled at the bald woman staring back at me. I expected this moment to be a traumatic event that would slice me to the bone and leave a permanent scar— but in DeAndre's care, it was the happiest I'd felt in weeks.

* * *

Two days later, I left our apartment for the first time since losing my hair. My family had sent me a collection of floral headscarves from my chemotherapy wish list, and I'd looked up YouTube tutorials to learn how to tie them. I wrapped a black headscarf with a red rose pattern around my bald head. I looked through my closet for the most neutral outfit, hoping to appear near-invisible out in the world, and settled on a black cotton maxi dress. Hiding my eyes behind sunglasses, I walked out the door, leaving the comforting confines of home.

My heart began to race as I walked through the lobby and out the front door of our building. My eyes darted in every direction, expecting to see people staring at me with confusion or disgust on their faces. I hoped my scarf would look like a fashion statement instead of a cancer cover-up, but I wasn't fooling anyone into believing I had hair underneath.

I drove to a wig shop I'd found through Yelp. It was a Monday afternoon, so the shop was quiet inside with only one or two other customers. I picked out some wigs, and the salesperson helped me try them on in front of the mirror. I was leaning toward wavy and curly wigs, styles that were reminiscent of the hair I had lost. This was a fruitless endeavor, though—every wig made me look like a beauty pageant reject. I didn't have the budget for a human hair wig, and most of the synthetic styles were comically voluminous, the thick strands shining like polished plastic. I tried on 10 different wigs before I settled on two—a dark chocolate brown bob with blunt bangs, and a medium brown wig with long, loose waves.

When I got home, I took out the long, wavy wig from the shopping bag and pulled it onto my head. I straightened the thick edges in the bathroom mirror, lining it up with my natural hairline, and ran my fingers through the length of the silky strands. Without giving myself time to change my mind, I flicked off the bathroom light and left our apartment to walk to H&M a few blocks away—a spin around the neighborhood to show off my temporary new look.

I made eye contact with the doorman in the lobby of our building and I started walking faster out the door, as if it would lead me through a portal where no one could see me.

I walked into H&M and went straight to the accessories corner. It was spring, the temperatures outside consistently warm, but that didn't deter me from putting two knit beanie hats in my basket. I found a women's baseball style hat and tried it on. It barely fit over the thick wig, but I put it in my basket anyway, along with a silk scarf. I walked around the store, weaving through the clothes racks. I was sure there were eyes following me from every direction. I started to sweat under the wig, my temperature rising as my humiliation soared. I quickly paid for my items and left.

When I got outside, I pulled on a black beanie over my wig. With sunglasses, a shiny plastic wig, and a black winter cap in the middle of L.A. spring, I probably looked like I was about to rob a bank.

No one prepared me for this. I was comfortable at home and at the doctor's office, where it was acceptable to look like a cancer patient. Out in the world, though, I felt like a freak. DeAndre assured me that the stares were probably imagined, delusions manifested from my profound insecurities. Maybe I had imagined them, but it didn't change the sweat that warmed my palms when I was out in public, or the way my face burned every time someone looked in my general direction.

I put the wigs away. They didn't bring me the sense of security I'd hoped they would—quite the opposite, actually. Also, they itched like hell. After all that, I ended up spending most days wrapped in my $8 scarves.

* * *

As I prepared for my second chemotherapy infusion, I decided to experiment in an effort to reduce some of the horrendous side effects. A friend I met on Instagram, who was also going through chemo, told me she fasted before each appointment. She pointed me to some research from a biologist at the University of Southern California who was studying the effects of fasting during chemotherapy. The articles I read suggested that fasting for 36 hours before chemotherapy and 24 hours after may potentially leave cancer cells more vulnerable while protecting healthy cells. My new friend told me that she had minimized her chemo side effects by doing this.

For two days before my next appointment, I sustained myself on bone broth, leafy green vegetable juice, and water. I showed up to my second chemo appointment with a peach floral scarf wrapped around my now completely hairless head. Four boring hours and two chemotherapy doses later, we were headed home to await more misery.

I woke up a few days later, on what should have been the onset of another hefty batch of terrible chemo side effects, feeling no worse than mildly under the weather. I practically danced out of the bedroom into the kitchen to make breakfast, a small chore I wasn't capable of after my first round of chemo.

"Can you believe this? I feel fine!" I shouted at DeAndre.

My bones still throbbed from the injections, there was no escaping that. Even so, I had a steady stream of energy and I was in good spirits as I took walks around the neighborhood and even went to a few extra yoga classes.

* * *

I spent the next two weeks preparing for Madeline's retreat. What does one pack for a spiritual retreat? I had no idea, certain I would be the odd one out if I didn't arrive in a tie-dye smock dress and Birkenstocks, items I did not own. I stuck with black leggings and a variety of oversized wool shawls, my go-to comfort clothes. I wrapped my favorite crystals in a scarf and packed them, along with my journal and various head coverings, in a backpack.

Gretchen flew in from New York the day before the retreat so that we could drive up together. The car rental agency assigned us a Kia *Soul,* which absolutely delighted me—a *Soul* to carry *my* battered and bruised soul up north. We hit the road as the sun came up on Thursday morning. Our destination, a retreat house with no address.

We arrived in the early evening at *Flowing Waters Retreat Center*, a large house with no cellphone service and no WiFi, sitting against a lively creek and surrounded by trees. Every detail was in stark contrast to my everyday life amidst the noise of downtown L.A. and heavily reliant on technology and screen time. The moment we turned into the driveway, I was thrust into the unfamiliar quiet of a disconnected existence.

angels

Gretchen and I walked through the wooden double doors into a symphony of laughter and friendly chatter. Aromas of cinnamon and cardamom traveled from the kitchen, weaving through the warm air and permeating the whole house. Madeline led us down the hall to a large room with three twin beds and windows up to the cathedral ceiling overlooking the flowing creek behind the property. We put our bags down and unpacked our clothes, wrapping shawls and sweaters over hangers in the closet, stacking folded leggings inside of dresser drawers.

Madeline had left an envelope on each of our pillows with a personal note and an oracle card. My card had the phrase "New Beginnings" at the top with a picture of a Banksia wildflower—an orange and yellow cone-shaped flower with small, spiked petals. Underneath the photo, it read, *Take this as an opportunity to rise from the ashes stronger and more determined.*

We made brief introductions and sat around the dining room table for an orientation with the owner of the property, who showed us how to catch and release a scorpion if we found one in the house (excuse me, what?) and assigned each of us a cloth napkin for the weekend (yes, you read that right). After we enjoyed our first home-cooked meal together that evening—roasted and charred sweet potatoes, chickpeas, and sautéed kale, all drizzled with tahini dressing—we gathered in a sacred circle in a small space just steps from the retreat house.

Madeline spread out 13 *Divine Feminine Oracle* cards face down in front of her. After settling into my spot in the circle, I crawled toward the cards, reached for the one I was most pulled to, and turned it over. The image on the card was of a woman with one breast exposed. Her name was Akhilanda, also known as "The Goddess of Never Not Broken." I read more about her in the oracle deck's booklet, and I learned that we often meet this Goddess when we are in our darkest moments of grief and heartbreak. She represents the essence of the phoenix rising from the ashes. I opened my journal to tuck the card away, and I saw the oracle card Madeline had left on my pillow. I'd already forgotten what it said. *Take this as an opportunity to rise from the ashes stronger and more determined.*

"Oh my god," I whispered.

One by one, we went around the circle and shared why we felt called to the retreat. I was already gushing tears when it came to my turn. I opened up about my miscarriages, how I was currently in the trenches being treated for breast cancer, and how I longed to be a mother after so much loss. We wrapped ourselves in blankets and sipped mugs of hot herbal tea as Madeline guided us through journal prompts. We partnered up and shared intimate details with strangers who would quickly become friends. Around 9 p.m., we slid on our shoes and walked across the damp grass back into the house.

* * *

Early the next morning, while most of the house was still asleep, Gretchen and I tiptoed out to the kitchen to pour ourselves coffee. Madeline told everyone the night before that she'd be leading optional Kundalini practice at 7:30 a.m. each morning of the retreat. I didn't want to miss out on a single offering, so I'd planned to attend every practice even though I had never experienced Kundalini before.

Five of us spread out in a circle in the space next to the house, and Madeline led us through a few minutes of cat-cow to warm up our bodies. On all fours, we raised our backs slowly into a high arch while our heads hung down, then lowered our spines into a curve as we turned our faces upward—arching and curving and breathing for the next few minutes until my spine was loose and my mind was wide awake.

"I'm feeling called," Madeline began, then paused for a moment. "I'm not sure why but I feel called to do this healing meditation."

She showed us how to get into the proper pose for the meditation—seated on the floor cross-legged with our elbows tucked against our rib cages. Our forearms were extended 45 degrees, and our palms were stretched flat and facing up with our fingers pressed together.

"The chant is 'Ra Ma Da Sa, Sa Say So Hung,'" she said. "On 'Hung,' pull your bellybutton in quickly. Close your eyes and we'll begin."

Madeline started the audio, soft instrumental music that we chanted over in unison. The sound of our voices layered with the music was ethereal, and it brought on a sensation of deep nostalgia. It reminded me of hearing a beloved song from my childhood, every beat dripping with vivid memories—the way my heart expands, chills dance across my skin, bliss rushes through my body like dopamine.

A minute into the chant, tears began pouring out of my eyes. The curves of my lashes held my heavy teardrops and I squeezed my eyes closed tightly to force them to fall. Eleven minutes later, when the meditation ended, my face was soaking wet from the intensely potent, yet gentle emotional purge.

"Holy shit, that was incredible," I whispered to Gretchen. I wiped my wet face with my sleeves before we stood up to head back into the house.

Before I stepped through the sliding glass door, I pulled Madeline aside. "I think I know why you felt called to lead us in that meditation. I think that was for me," I said.

Madeline's blue eyes lit up and she smiled. "I had a feeling it might be for you."

* * *

That afternoon, Madeline planned an excursion for the group. It had been lightly raining all morning, and after my morning meditation—which left me feeling like I'd just had an eight-hour therapy session—I was content to relax indoors, my belly full of homemade granola and fresh berries. I didn't sign up to sit on the sidelines, though, so I pulled on two layers of leggings and a hoodie before stepping out into the chilly, wet Mount Shasta air.

Thirteen of us piled into three cars and we drove to a remote location on the mountain. The rain was coming down harder when we arrived, so we pulled giant garbage bags over our bodies and tore holes with our cold fingers for our arms and heads to poke through. Draped in black makeshift rain ponchos, we walked through the tall, damp trees, each decorated with fluorescent green moss. Fog floated above us as plump raindrops sprinkled down.

We came to a clearing surrounded by fallen tree trunks, and we put our backpacks down. Our retreat chef, Revanna, distributed individual lunch containers packed with quinoa salad she'd prepared that morning. We scooped her homemade hummus into our bowls and dipped carrot spears and bell pepper slices, all of it getting wet.

I didn't sign up to the retreat to sit on the sidelines, but I also didn't sign up to learn how to survive the wilderness, to make a raincoat out of a garbage bag, endure muddy hikes, and eat wet quinoa salad. No, I longed to be warm and cozy in the car with the heater on high, or better yet, back at the house with my feet by the fireplace, humming along to Fleetwood Mac. As we finished lunch and put our containers away, Madeline stood in the center of the group.

"I want to honor each of you for being here," she said. "By showing up to this retreat, you're showing up for yourselves. We're out here on the mountain, and I know it's cold and rainy. It would be so much easier to be inside where it's comfortable." She placed both her hands over her heart and glanced at each of our faces. "I commend each and every one of you for showing up, even in the storms."

* * *

Mount Shasta is often called a place "where heaven and Earth meet," and it is said that the veil between realms is much thinner there. I didn't know this prior to arriving, but it became clear as messages began showing up for me, and I could only interpret them as divine. In our sacred circles, I always spoke of motherhood. Almost every journal prompt, partner activity, and playlist during breathwork brought me face-to-face with my dream of having a child. The more I spoke out loud about my desire to be a mother and the ache that plagued me in the absence of my children, the closer I felt to them.

During breath healing one afternoon, lying on the ground with my eyes closed, I saw a vision of a woman with angel wings. She was holding hands with a small child. Their figures were rich navy shadows, but they glistened like the Mount Shasta night sky that I'd fallen in love with on day one—completely saturated with stars. The child turned around, twisting her body toward me without letting go of the woman's hand. I saw my hands appear in my periphery. I was reaching out to her, begging for her to stay, but they were already fading. I thanked her for visiting me, and I watched them disappear.

I didn't share this story with anyone else until more than a year later. When my mom read an early draft of this chapter, she emailed me.

*I believe your woman with angel wings is my angel,
the one who came to me in my dream to let me know
you wanted to be born.*

I called my mom and asked her to tell me the story again. My parents had three children by late 1979, my two brothers and sister. They closed that chapter, decided they were done and that their family was complete. When my sister was around two-years-old, my mom dreamed of a baby girl named Mary Catherine. Mary is my mother's name, and Catherine is her mother's middle name. She woke my dad up with urgency and told him that she thinks they gave Gretchen the wrong name and that they should have named her Mary Catherine. My dad was bewildered by her sudden, panicked realization. He told her that they would not be changing Gretchen's name and not to worry about it—it was just a dream. A few months later, their attempt at natural family planning failed, and she found out she was pregnant. As the story goes, she knew all along that it was a girl, and she knew her name would be Mary Catherine.

My mom told me this story often, from a young age, and I repeated it to anyone who would listen. "My mom had a dream about me before I was born. She already knew my name. She didn't even need to go to the doctor, she knew she was pregnant with a girl because she dreamed of me," I'd say with a smug smile, exaggerating extra details without ever asking if they were accurate. I couldn't believe I never knew there was an angel in her dream.

After she shared that with me, I imagined stories that, perhaps, I'd tell my own child one day. Gazing at soft, closed eyelids, head resting in the crook of my elbow. I'd whisper, "You came to me in a dream." Maybe when they're a bit older, I'd snuggle them close to me at bedtime and tell them, "An angel once brought you to me, but you weren't ready yet. We met long before you were born." And they will know that they've lived in my heart for years, long before this moment, tucked under cozy blankets as they drift off to sleep.

* * *

Mount Shasta has a permanent home in my heart—mossy tree trunks, velvet fog, starry skies, and new friendships live there. I'd shed an entire identity within Mount Shasta's borders, the ashes of my former self spread out on the earth, resting in the leaves, and swirling through the mountain air. By the end of the retreat, I was so changed, I barely recognized the woman I was on the first night, curled up in the darkest shadows of my soul. The emotional baggage I'd collected over the past few years was loads lighter, and my heart was overflowing with so much joy, I wanted to sing in the faces of strangers and shout at everyone everywhere I went, "You are magnificent and I love you!" For what felt like the first time in my life, I was receiving an invitation to spread my wings—so I vowed to do just that as I integrated back into everyday life.

On Monday morning, after many heartfelt goodbyes, we headed back to L.A. where more chemo awaited me. As soon as we reached an area with cell service, I logged into Facebook and held my thumb on that button I'd hovered over so many times, finally leaving the cancer support groups.

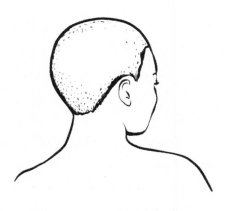

brave

My third chemotherapy session was scheduled for the day after I returned from Mount Shasta. Because of the long drive back to L.A., and my desire for more of Revanna's homemade granola on that last morning of the retreat, I decided not to fast beforehand.

I wore my long wig and a thick, black and white abstract patterned headband around my forehead, which prompted DeAndre to ask me if I'd joined an 80s hair band over the weekend. I still hadn't acquired a tie-dyed smock dress and Birkenstocks, but I was getting closer.

Gretchen and I stopped for açai bowls and mixed green juice from the juice bar across the street from the hospital before checking in to the oncology department. This third session marked halfway through my chemo regimen. We decided to celebrate the milestone the same way we celebrated most life events—with pizza!

That evening, we sat in a maroon vinyl booth and traded slices of piping hot brick oven pizza. I stared off into space as I savored fresh, melted mozzarella and house made red sauce, knowing I would not be able to taste these flavors a week from now. As I nibbled on the last chewy morsel of pizza crust, fatigue began to creep up on me, my eyelids becoming heavy, and brain fog rolling in. We drove Gretchen to the airport where she got on a plane back to New York, and I went home and promptly crawled into bed.

* * *

The side effects hit me like a freight train this time, worsening by the hour—body aches, nausea, all the while lying on damp sheets from endless hot flashes.

Three days after my infusion, I woke up with chills. I reached for the thermometer on my nightstand and slid it under my tongue as I lay sweaty—and on the verge of tears—under the covers. I had a 101-degree fever. I wrapped myself in extra blankets to ease the chills, and rested a cool, wet washcloth on my forehead to bring my fever down. DeAndre came into the room once or twice every hour to check my water cup, and delicately order me to stay hydrated, but I couldn't swallow a single sip of anything without heaving.

The washcloth brought my fever down some hours later and I was able to nap through the evening. When I woke up around 9 p.m., my body was both boiling and shivering. I held the thermometer under my tongue, my eyes glossy as the intense misery stretched beyond my breaking point. My fever had climbed above 102-degrees. The sweat seeping out of my pores wreaked, the rancid, medicinal chemo smell so severe that I wanted to peel my skin off.

I lay folded over in bed, my face buried in blankets, and listened as DeAndre dialed the nurse hotline.

"Yeah, she's right here," he said. He tapped the speakerphone button and held the phone near my face.

"Am I speaking to Mary?" the nurse asked.

"Yes," I replied just barely above a whisper.

"So, I'm going to recommend that you go to the emergency room tonight," she said, her voice gentle but firm.

I opened my mouth to respond, but the words that escaped my lips were incoherent, a stream of sounds that one would expect from a wounded puppy.

"Oh," the nurse moaned. Her voice washed over me, a warm wave of loving sympathy. "I know that's not what you wanted to hear. I'm sorry."

"It's okay. Thank you." I managed to squeak out those few words before burying my face in blankets to weep as I gathered the energy required to put clothes on.

I weakly pulled on a pair of black sweatpants, a black beanie, and a gray hoodie. I slowly stepped down the hall, into the elevator, and out the front lobby door where DeAndre was waiting with the car.

At the hospital check-in desk, I handed my ID to the receptionist. "Hello," I said. I tried to smile but my face hurt as much as the rest of my body. "I'm in the middle of cancer treatment and I have a fever." I crossed my fingers that these details would bump me to the top of the waitlist so that I could go home as soon as possible, and thankfully, they did—a nurse called my name a few minutes later.

I climbed into the hospital bed and reluctantly took off my beanie as I reclined back, resting my head on a small white pillow. I never wanted anyone other than DeAndre to see my bald head. The way that people who knew me looked at me now that I was visibly ill—the subtle push-out of their lower lip and the gentle furrow of their brow—made me feel like they were already planning my funeral in their minds. My forehead and cheeks were glistening with sweat from the warm knit fabric, though, so I plucked off my hat and placed it in my lap.

The nurse jabbed my hand with a needle and hooked up an IV to replenish my fluids. They brought in a portable X-ray machine to check my lungs for pneumonia, took a few vials of blood, and examined me further for other signs of infection. My fever came down within the hour, all the tests came back clear, and I was discharged just after midnight.

DeAndre dropped me off in front of our building and said he was going to go find something to eat. Since he'd spent his entire day closely monitoring me, he missed the window for dinner. I waved away his offer to bring me food. My sights were set on one thing only—crawling into bed and sleeping for the next two days.

I walked toward our building with a bright white medical mask over my face, hiding my pasty bald head under my hoodie. I kept my head down as I walked past groups of tipsy young people in high heels gathering in front of our building. They were flirting, exchanging phone numbers, touching up lipstick, and talking about which bar to go to next. My envy over their freedom manifested as rage in my belly that quickly turned to self-pity. I pulled my hoodie forward, my face a blurred shadow in the cave of fabric, and got on the elevator.

I was getting ready to lie down when I heard the door open 20 minutes later, but I wasn't tired anymore. The hydrating IV swept through my veins like a double espresso, and I was wide awake when DeAndre walked in with a salami sub in his hand. My appetite returned the second I smelled mustard smeared on top of salty salami, pickles, and black olives on fluffy white bread. DeAndre side-eyed me salivating over his sandwich and asked me if I wanted a bite. I stood over him as I chewed my one perfect bite and watched him unwrap the other half, dumping a small bag of Hot Cheetos onto the spread out paper wrapper.

I observed his every move as if I was circling my prey, waiting for the right moment to pounce. "I know I said I wasn't hungry, but can I have another bite?" I asked with an apologetic smile.

We did this dance for two more bites before he groaned and handed me half his sandwich. I was entranced as I watched him set the small tower of bread, meat, and cheese in front of me, because nothing in my life had *ever* tasted as delicious as that 2 a.m. post-emergency room sandwich.

* * *

For the next two weeks, I spent every waking hour moping around the apartment. I whined to DeAndre, and when he wasn't around to hear me, I whined out loud to no one. "I can't do this three more times. I just can't. This is hell."

I was on the verge of tears as my fourth chemotherapy appointment neared. My resistance was a giant knot in my stomach, rope tethered to my chest—a tug-of-war in my body as I became more desperate to find a way to break out of this nightmare.

212

During my fourth chemotherapy infusion, my oncologist came by my chair to check on me as the liquid medicine poured through my IV tube. She usually spent a few minutes with me during these long appointments, but sometimes her busy schedule didn't allow it and I was left in the care of the wonderful nurses. She pulled up a stool next to my chair and shared that she had some news to tell me. I braced myself for bad news—a side effect of having cancer—instinctively protecting myself from disappointment by expecting the worst news imaginable.

"I wanted to tell you that a new study was just published. Based on your diagnosis, any further chemotherapy will be unnecessary. The harm of six treatments would outweigh the benefits. Today will be your last chemo treatment," she explained.

My eyes were big, my face wrinkled like a pug puppy as she finished speaking. I lowered my head and cried. She smiled and patted my hand before standing up to leave.

Tears poured down my face as I typed a message to my family group chat, my thumbs shaky from the massive adrenaline hit: *LAST CHEMO!!!* DeAndre took a photo of me with my arms in the air in celebration—a cautious, delicate victory pose because the clear IV tube was still sticking out of my forearm—and uploaded it to the group chat.

* * *

As the final dose of chemo drugs knocked me on my ass one last time before leaving my system for good, my eyebrows and eyelashes started to thicken again, and the hair on my head began to sprout. In two weeks' time, I went from a few stray hairs on top of my head—think Tommy Pickles—to G.I. Jane, a deep brown five o'clock shadow covering my head.

It was late July and hot as hell in L.A. when I stepped out of the bedroom, fully dressed in black skinny jeans and a red and white striped fitted T-shirt, ready to go out one afternoon. No scarf, no hat, no wig. DeAndre glanced at me, then did a double-take.

"You're going out like that?" he asked.

Those few words made me second-guess myself. I turned on my heels to go back into the room and re-evaluate my decision.

"Hey!" DeAndre stopped me. "Good for you. I'm proud of you," he said.

I stayed glued to DeAndre's arm as we walked outside. I noticed people staring, which unnerved me, my stomach flipping every time I felt someone's gaze land on me. Being out in public with a buzz-cut made me feel like I was performing the role of cancer survivor, and even the tiniest hint of attention was mortifying. I pulled myself closer to DeAndre, trying to merge us into one body. He was my security blanket, a shield to hide my vulnerabilities as I put them on display in the bright light of day.

The next afternoon, we were out running errands when DeAndre got an urgent work-related email. He looked up from his phone, turned to me, and said, "Meet back at home?"

A surge of heat rushed through my body at the mere suggestion of walking four blocks without my security blanket, my protector.

"Um, are you sure?" I asked, as if my clothes were unraveling from my body and I was about to be standing naked in the chip aisle of Whole Foods.

"You got this," DeAndre said.

I know he was talking about the cheese and crackers in my basket, but I took those three words to heart. *Fuck yes, I got this.* Fifteen minutes later, I darted out of Whole Foods and walked home as fast as I could, brushing beads of nervous sweat from my neck as I stepped onto the elevator and exhaled. *Ah, I did it.*

As my hair grew, covering more of my pasty white scalp, so did my bravery for being out in public. Actually, bravery is an understatement. I embodied supreme badass. No longer mortified by every pair of eyes that glanced in my general direction, I embraced my public persona of cancer survivor, or whatever assumptions others made about my appearance. At times, I relished the mystery that was associated with having my hair so short. I imagined people being interested in my buzz-cut origin story, asking themselves, *Did she shave her head in the middle of an existential crisis? Does she have an illness? Or is she just rebelling against painfully long hair routines?* I was so smug parading my skull around, my hair short and silky like kitten fur.

Of course, for a shy, self-conscious introvert like me, there were downsides to looking "unconventional." DeAndre and I were in Target one day picking out a toy for my nephew when a small child walked by us, looked at me, and asked his dad loudly, "Is that a boy or a girl?" I didn't hold it against the child, but I did wish he'd used his inside voice so I wouldn't have gotten my feelings hurt.

A week later, I was walking home from the grocery store with heavy bags in each hand. I was just around the corner from our building when I heard someone yell, "SINEAD! SINEAD!" followed by hysterical laughter.

It took a beat for me to realize he was yelling this entirely unoriginal joke—and supposed insult—at me. I stopped abruptly and swung my body around, my grocery bags banging into my legs. I saw the shirtless asshole sitting on the ledge of some landscaping in front of an office building. Standing next to him was someone I recognized, a guy who lived in my apartment building and with whom I'd rode the elevator many times. They were smoking weed, passing a glass pipe between them.

"Is that supposed to be funny?" I asked. The man looked at me with a shit-eating grin, unfazed. "I HAD CANCER, YOU ASSHOLE. Is it still funny?" I raised my arms a few inches, weighed down by heavy grocery bags, but a necessary gesture to emphasize my rage, my unwillingness to be fucked with.

My neighbor looked like a deer in headlights as he shook his head and quietly answered, "No."

I turned around and kept walking, my heart beating fast as adrenaline flooded my body. I don't know what I expected from confronting that man—as if he was open to receiving a lesson in kindness, as if it was worth risking my safety to scream mean things at him. Still, my words roaring through my throat and shooting off the tip of my tongue felt like spitting fiery arrows through the sky, impaling my enemy.

The next day, I walked into the elevator, and my neighbor, who had witnessed my fury, was standing inside.

"Oh. Hi," I said. "Who's your friend?"

He looked up from his phone and his eyes grew wide. "Oh my god, I am *so* sorry about that. I don't know that guy, I was smoking outside, and he asked for a hit," he explained.

"Huh, okay. Well, maybe next time, speak up," I said. I crossed my arms and turned to face the door.

He apologized again. Every time I saw him after that, he went out of his way to be overly nice to me—cheerfully greeting me by name, asking me how my day was, complimenting my hair as it grew and the ends began to curl.

* * *

A few weeks after chemotherapy ended, I started daily radiation therapy. I was tattooed with four tiny blue dots in a diamond shape around my left breast to guide the radiation therapist to the same exact area at each appointment. I drove 20 minutes to the hospital every weekday morning for appointments that lasted less than five minutes, and I did this for four consecutive weeks.

Spending mornings in the radiation department felt like a special ritual. There was an understated sense of community in the waiting room—I could feel it when I walked in, the comfort of a cool breeze kissing my skin in the middle of summer. Not everyone chatted with each other, I certainly didn't, as a quiet observer—but I understood that, in a sense, these were my people. By the fourth week, it was as familiar as walking into grandma's house for Christmas Eve dinner.

There was one patient, a man who appeared to be in his forties, who gave everyone his attention when they walked in and greeted each person with kindness when their eyes met his. He talked to people sitting nearby, his voice emanating throughout the large waiting room. One morning, he said, "We're all so strong," referring to everyone in the room—all of us whose names would appear on the large waiting room monitor, assigning us a radiation room each day. We'd sit and stare at the screen, waiting for bright green pixels in the shape of our names to pop up.

Purdie, M... 4B.

When I saw my name, I'd walk through the corridor to the changing area, grab a gown from the cupboard, and head to my assigned room to be zapped quickly and sent home. I sulked briefly when my radiation ended, knowing I would miss those tender strangers with whom I spent a few sweet minutes each day.

hurdles

In late August, a week after my last radiation appointment, I began daily medication—the final piece of my treatment, the little white pill that caused my heart to plummet into my feet when the surgeon told me I'd need to take it for more than five years, in the same breath wrecking my plans to have a baby anytime soon. After the retreat, though, I'd surrendered to the idea of divine timing, the belief that it'll happen when it's meant to, the belief that something bigger is at play and I am to simply put one foot in front of the other and trust—until that, too, began to waver.

My patience had a shelf-life of only a few months. I was reaching my arms toward a nothingness, a fading dream that only felt further away with each passing day. After every miscarriage, visions of the future were still vivid—telling stories huddled under bedsheets draped over the backs of chairs while chocolate chip cookies cool on the kitchen counter, slow bike rides around the neighborhood as training wheels squeak and the sun begins to set against an orange and pink sky, Saturdays quietly pacing the aisles of the library to find another marvelous story.

These images were blurred outlines on worn, crumpled paper now, smudged pencil marks left behind by an oily pink eraser. We had no resources, no plans, no timeline. The unknown was bleak, and I began to slip away from myself as I gave way to existential dread. I questioned why I was here, and why there was so much pain and suffering along my path. *Haven't I learned enough? Can I have my dreams now? What else has to happen?* I longed to experience the sweet serenity of indifference—how much easier it would be if only I didn't want this so damn much.

I began filling our kitchen with an abundance of Ben & Jerry's pints and bottles of wine, reliable distractions that I'd used for most of my adult life to both comfort me and offer an escape from whatever emotions I didn't want to sit with. My beloved yoga classes became a distant memory, embarrassed to show up as my leggings and cotton tank tops became uncomfortably tight on my body. My once cherished nightly bath-time ritual sounded less appealing and more exhausting—it cut into my 10 p.m. ice cream eating hour, anyway, so no thank you.

Every day, I got out of bed and threw myself a pity-party. I dragged my heels around the apartment like Eeyore, moping about my body changing, whining that as long as I was stuck in limbo—post-cancer and pre-motherhood—my life lacked direction and purpose. Nothing stung more than looking ahead toward a foggy future, not having a single fucking clue what was going to happen, nor what I should be doing in the meantime besides twiddle my thumbs and feel sorry for myself.

I was talking on the phone to Michelle, lamenting my latest struggles, when something shifted.

"I don't know, I just don't even see the point of doing all that deep self-care anymore. I was way more motivated before because we were trying to get pregnant. Like, completely invested in doing everything right by my body to benefit my future baby. But now I just feel like—I'm not going to be pregnant, so it's becoming harder to keep it up," I said.

"Everything you do to take care of yourself now will benefit your baby, Mary," Michelle said.

Of course. I knew this, and yet I needed to hear the words out loud for the door to finally open—warm light leaking in through the entryway, inviting me out of my victimhood mindset. I owed it to myself to do more than bathe in pity, waiting to become someone's mother, even through the longest days when the void seemed so gaping that I could hardly tolerate facing it. I was craving instant gratification, desperate to reap the rewards of my—at one time—intense commitment to self-care, forgetting that sacred self-care is a long game. I deserved better than to treat my body like a toxic dumping ground, repeating old destructive patterns and deceiving myself into believing I was powerless against them.

I invited in grace, refusing to punish myself for struggling. Grace asked me to stop placing blame and instead to listen, breathe, and pause. Grace didn't demand that I implement hard rules for my body, only suggested that I approach food and movement with intention. Grace reminded me how much I adored everything I had denied myself—preparing a wholesome meal from scratch with love, putting pen to paper in the mornings to clear my mind, wandering local hiking trails with a sweet playlist humming through my earphones, sipping herbal tea in the evenings as flames sway softly on top of lavender scented candles. The teeter-totter I had been sitting on the past several months, with my ass in the dirt, finally started to level out.

There was a time when I believed I was so in control, I had years planned out in advance. If a family member invited us on a vacation that was 11 months away, I'd become agitated. *We can't book a vacation, we're going to have a newborn to take care of!* How many experiences did

I miss out on because my planning brain built barriers around my life? I did not go through hell just to sit and sulk until the next good thing happened. Every day was bubbling over with good things, and the fog was finally clearing so that I could see them.

* * *

As soon as my active treatment began to wind down, DeAndre signed up to be a volunteer mentor through Big Brothers and Big Sisters of Los Angeles. Twice a month, he spent an entire day with his 10-year-old Little Brother. DeAndre took his role seriously, usually fretting over what to do to make their days together memorable. He would come home glowing after a day of playing basketball in the park, or watching an NBA game at Staples Center. They always went out to eat, sometimes to a movie, and when his birthday was nearing, DeAndre took him to the mall and let him pick out new sneakers.

Witnessing DeAndre step into his Big Brother role with such care naturally fueled my yearning for a child. The anxiety and impatience that usually accompanied this yearning were absent, though. This so-called pause that I resented so deeply was actually a gift, an opportunity to slow down and observe all the ways we can turn off auto-pilot within ourselves and live—*truly live* with heartfelt intention—through the unwelcome delay.

* * *

In October, I found out that the startup I had been designing for part-time for more than a year was at risk of going out of business. This meant they were laying off the few remaining employees, myself included.

Since my first reading with Michelle almost a year ago, I'd been focused on creating and sharing art from the depths of my heart—less concerned with how I could monetize it and solely interested in making people feel something. Michelle would often remind me, "Keep making art for art's sake!" This relieved some of the pressure I felt about making a living out of my creative passion. When I worried about the audience, critiquing art in terms of "shareability" or wondering if a piece would sell, my oasis of creativity turned into a drought. Making art for art's sake gave me the kind of creative freedom I had as a child, when I created *The Lost Puppy* because the story was on my heart, not because I was planning to put a price tag on it.

Because I'd been persistent with this—strengthening my creative skills, sharpening my illustration style, and regularly sharing art on Instagram—I'd grown a following of around 20,000 over the past year. Though social media was often a sore spot, personally speaking, it was suddenly opening doors for me professionally, and my freelance illustration career began picking up momentum after my employment ended at the startup.

My first big commission was from a well-known agency who emailed me out of the blue and asked me to design and illustrate a mural for a chewing gum company. The mural would be displayed on the Venice Beach boardwalk for four weeks. I screamed when I got the email, thrilled that someone would ask me to create something that would be seen by the masses—and pay me for it! I illustrated lemon slices and mint leaves riding the surf, bright blue beach waves curling across the horizontal frame against a group of palm trees and a pastel sunset sky.

Creative opportunities began to snowball over the next few months. I had accepted a temporary retail position over the holidays after I was laid off, but I was forced to quit after two months because I was up to my neck in freelance work. Between December and February, I went from helping people pick out eyeglass frames in an upscale mall 35 hours a week to creating artwork for some of my favorite brands—social illustrations for the dating website where I'd met DeAndre almost nine years earlier, editorial illustrations for a story on miscarriage and baby loss published on an international news site, and cover art for a few popular podcasts. When those projects ended, more brands and agencies reached out to me before I could even think about my next move. I was hired for a temporary in-house gig with a major pop culture brand, two book illustration commissions, and one live-drawing event where I bombed so hard the embarrassment still makes me cringe (hey, you can't win 'em all).

I was living the dream I'd given up on three years earlier, a dream that I thought was impossible to achieve so far into my seemingly "failed" career. Even when I was working long, late hours, hunched over my desk after midnight to meet a deadline, I was overflowing with gratitude for this life.

Some journeys are thousands of miles long, dragging us through the deepest valleys and over the sharpest peaks. I was never meant to rush through, nor was I meant to step off the path when I tripped over a hurdle. Perhaps rejection isn't a dead end or a WRONG WAY sign, but rather a waiting room, a cozy seat in a rose garden with honey lattés and fresh baked cookies. Maybe what we view as rejection is simply an invitation to exercise patience—a promise that something better is on the way.

My only regret is believing my life was supposed to look a certain way by a certain time, a belief that clouded my vision and kept me from slowing down sooner to savor all the beautiful experiences, however seemingly insignificant, that brought me to this very moment. This moment, always exactly where I am supposed to be.

rainbows

DeAndre and I were sitting by a hotel pool in Cabo San Lucas, Mexico, when I got an email from Madeline. It was mid-May, a year since the retreat, and she had just opened enrollment for the next Mount Shasta retreat in the fall. Elation permeated my bones just as it had on the morning I woke up to Madeline's invitation 14 months earlier. My belly full of Prosecco and fish tacos, I clicked the link and reserved my spot.

In September, Gretchen and I returned to Mount Shasta together. Living on separate coasts, this was becoming our new favorite tradition. Our girls' trips used to look like bottomless mimosas, sleeping late, and ordering greasy breakfast burritos to combat all-day hangovers. Now our girls' trips included late-night stargazing with our hands wrapped around mugs of hot tea, early morning yoga, and sitting on pillows by the fireplace eating homemade vegan desserts until our bellies were full.

We arrived on a Thursday afternoon, this time at a different retreat house with no scorpions and 13 new friends. Red and orange leaves crackled under our bare feet as we walked through the dewy grass, exploring the property. Large wooden stalls were off to one side, two outdoor showers nestled under tall trees. Cozy gray couches curved around the living room, facing large windows and the door to the back deck where we'd eat most meals, soak in the afternoon sun, and wrap ourselves in blankets to gaze up at a million twinkling stars at night.

We gathered in the front room of the house for the opening circle that night. I'd been thinking all day about what to say when I introduced myself to the group, channeling my annoying planning brain to avoid fumbling over my words.

"I want to try something different as we open the circle," Madeline said. "We'll go around the room and share, but I want you to begin with, 'If you really knew me, you'd know...'"

Moving clockwise around the circle, each person finished the sentence as they introduced themselves. Some delivered lengthy monologues, some offered only a single breadcrumb. For me, the sentence finished itself without a second thought.

"If you really knew me, you'd know that I'm a mother, even though you can't see my children."

* * *

During our first outing as a group the next day, Madeline took us to a familiar location on the mountain. We gathered in a circle in a vast open space in the middle of the forest, seated on blankets and mats brought from the retreat house. I took off my shoes and rested the soles of my feet on the cool, damp earth. Madeline led us in a nature oracle activity to connect with the elements around us.

Right away, I was pulled to an area directly behind me where two small trees demanded my attention. They were away from the other trees, side by side, and intertwined as if they were holding hands or dancing. To me, they looked like children playing.

I sat on a rock next to the playful pair and closed my eyes, hoping for an intuitive message to fall into my lap, perhaps a love note from the trees. A flock of birds flew overhead—flapping wings and high-pitched chirps pierced the mountain air. The damp dirt under my feet brought up sweet memories of making mud-pies with childhood friends, squatting in the backyard and shoveling gobs of thick mud into aluminum pie pans, pressing yellow dandelions around the edges for a bright finishing touch.

Ten minutes later, I blinked my eyes open slowly and stood up to walk back to the group. I walked 20 feet before stopping abruptly to turn around—I wanted a picture of my new nature friends. I opened the camera on my phone and pointed it at the trees. I glanced at the screen, awestruck. The light was wrapping the trees, creating a perfect arch over the top—a rainbow. I snapped two photos and looked at them closely to be sure I wasn't imagining it. The photo felt like a message, the light a messenger—my children, my future rainbow babies, were there with me in spirit.

* * *

On the second to last day of the retreat, we went as a group to a sacred location for a deep meditative experience. When we arrived, we each climbed up a steep wooden staircase, through a hatch, and into a pitch-black room with low, slanted ceilings. I crawled to one corner, wrapped my wool shawl close around my upper body, and closed my eyes. Thirteen breaths whistled quietly through the room.

About 10 minutes into the meditation, I heard music playing from somewhere in the back of my mind. As the melody became sharper, I realized the song was "Over the Rainbow," and it continued to play on a loop, lulling me into decadent relaxation like a warm bath. Tears seeped through the cracks of my closed eyes as I heard the lyrics, "That's where you'll find me…"

Back at the house, I sat face-to-face with Dillon, one of many beautiful friends I'd made on the retreat. As the weekend was coming to a close, Madeline encouraged us to partner up one last time and share our experiences from the day's activities. Dillon and I sat on green and purple mats on the hardwood floor as moonlight glowed through the French doors behind me.

"I had a really amazing experience today! During the meditation, I heard 'Over the Rainbow' playing, like, in my mind. And look at this," I said as I unlocked my phone. I pulled up the photo I'd taken of the rainbow arching over the trees a few days before and handed it to her. "It's like my children are telling me they're with me, you know? Just over the rainbow. And look, there they are! It's like I can feel them around me, and even though I haven't held them in my arms yet…"

Dillon looked up from the photo in her hands, her dark brown eyes locked with mine. Her words danced off her lips with urgency, interrupting me mid-sentence. "You think you haven't held them? Because I think you have," she said.

I was silent, marinating in her words. Then, tears dripped down my cheeks.

* * *

We left the retreat house the next morning and headed on the long journey home, stopping at a local market first. I was wandering around the small market, my arms full of road trip snacks—trail mix, chocolate, and bottled cold brew coffee. I was handing the items off to Gretchen when I heard my name, a familiar voice over the lively chatter of customers waiting in the deli line.

"Mary?"

I turned around and scanned a crowd of faces. April was smiling at me, her long, dark brown hair and sun-kissed skin just as I remembered from the first time we met.

My jaw dropped. "April! Oh my god!" I wove around customers and shopping carts, reaching over the elastic rope line divider to embrace her.

It had been nearly two years since I found her through an internet search, sitting in bed as my tender womb recovered from my last miscarriage. My Reiki session with April was the first stop on my healing journey after losing our baby girl, the first moment my heart began to open after days of clenched fists hitting pillows, screaming curse words while tears and snot ran down my face.

I left the market and slid into the passenger seat. Goosebumps tickled my arms as the message behind this unlikely run-in 600 miles from home was suddenly illuminated, a soft light flickering on in my awareness. April appeared like a small hand waving, or a perfect bow wrapping around every magical moment from that weekend—one last message for the road, sent to me from somewhere over the rainbow.

gifts

To my unborn child,

You were not the first to steal our hearts before vanishing so suddenly, but you left behind the deepest footprints, tiny round grooves on my ceiling that I stared at every night as I begged to understand why you had to leave. I dreamed of naming you Luz because you were our shining light after so many seasons of gray clouds and cold, pouring rain.

And then you were gone.

The stars stopped shining that day, and I wandered through the soul-crushing darkness in your absence, pleading with my angels to bring you back to me.

As pieces of my heart fell to the floor in that exam room, I asked to go with you, praying to be wherever you are. We had been so strong and endured so much before you came along. You were perfect. You were going to be the one that made it all the way into our arms.

In my dreams, I could hear your giggles as my fingertips dance lightly across your belly, and I'd do it again and again because the sound of your laughter is the sweetest medicine on Earth. I could feel your little body nestled against mine—your warm, wet cheeks cooling off as I hold you in the dark, my exhausted tears mixing with yours. And yet, every time I feel the weight of you in my arms, I am reminded that you are worth every tear I have ever shed, so I hum a lullaby for as long as it takes to rock you back to sleep. I could see you taking your first steps, bravely letting go of my hand, marching three triumphant steps, and stumbling into your daddy's arms while the whole room cheers for you.

I searched for meaning in the mess—a thousand glistening shards of my broken heart—desperate to understand why we were robbed of your light. Because of you, I embarked on the bumpy terrain toward healing. I wanted to be your mother so badly, and as I stepped on this path to mending my heart, you began showing me how to be a good mother to myself. You gave me that gift, even in your absence. As I healed, your light continued to pour through every crack in my heart.

Two months after we said goodbye to you, I was looking at myself in the mirror and noticed a lump in my left breast. A week later, the doctor called and told me I had breast cancer. I wondered, how could this happen? I'd taken huge strides toward healing, feeling you closer to me with every magnificent step, but cancer suddenly put my whole life in reverse. This body that I was trying so hard to care for, to forgive, to love, had betrayed me.

When I learned more about my diagnosis, it became tragically clear that losing you was the best-case scenario. The pregnancy hormones flooding my body would have encouraged the cancer to grow, possibly spread. If I'd carried you all nine months, would I have been around long enough to see you grow up? Would I have ever given myself the tender care and attention that led me to finding the lump? Guilt rushed through me as my gratitude blossomed. How could I be grateful for losing you? The answer landed in my mind—softly, like a feather falling to the grass.

My daughter, you saved my life.

The tenderness with which I began to love myself again, a side effect of losing you, was the reason I stared at my bare body in the mirror, forgiving myself for not being a better home to you. You were the reason I studied my silhouette, twirling slowly in front of the mirror every morning, reaching for kind words. Because of those quiet mornings alone with my reflection, I found the tumor and caught the cancer early. Because of you, I had a fighting chance. I'm receiving beautiful gifts packaged in sorrow, each wrapped in thick silky ribbons that shimmer in your light. I am learning what it means to be a mother —first to myself, and one day, to you too. The pain and beauty braided together, a cord connecting us between realms.

I understand now that you had to leave so that I could stay. You left your precious body behind that day to save me, but I know your spirit remains. I know that you hear my voice every time I speak to you. I can feel you close to me at night when I lay my head on my pillow and tell you that I miss you. I can feel your warmth every time I light a candle in your honor. My daughter, my heroine.

I love you.

acknowledgments

My husband, DeAndre, for choosing me every day and reminding me why I choose you forever. That psychic on our fourth date was right, you are my soulmate, and you make living through the worst days so much easier because your love carries me. Thank you for lifting me up as I wrote these words, encouraging me to share both our tough moments and our love, our messy heartbreak and our ongoing resilience. You are my everything.

Gretchen, my sister and my best friend in this life and no doubt many others. Thank you for your commitment to reading almost every goddamn revision of this book as it came together over the past two years. I hope to always be as good a sister to you as you have been to me for my whole life, but I'm not sure I could ever reach the level of sheer awesomeness that is reserved for badass big sisters like you. I love you!

Mom and dad, thank you for showing up for me and for us every step of the way. I know how much it hurts to witness your child endure so much, but I have made it out the other side because of your example of tenacity and your unwavering support. When you shared the dream story, you always told me, "There is a special reason you were born." I think this is part of that special reason, to create gifts out of my tremendous pain. It doesn't always make sense, but it can still be beautiful.

Jeremy, Paola, and Isaac, I cherish our time spent together between chemotherapy sessions. Thank you for taking my mind off of cancer during those fun day trips.

Bryan, Szilvia, and (the best cheerleaders!) Allegra and Arabella, thank you for rooting for me from an ocean away. Your handmade mail and our video chats never fail to brighten my days.

Jacqueline, my gateway into spiritual healing! Thank you for the long talks about herbal medicine and astrology. From Otis days to New York rooftops, L.A. hikes, breathwork, and pool days. I'm forever thankful that our paths crossed again. You are so special!

Madeline, I never imagined one evening of breath healing would change my life so much, but you've seen the evolution firsthand. Thank you for opening me up to the angelic realm, for facilitating my most memorable breath circles where I felt safe and held, and for introducing me to heaven on Earth: Mount Shasta. Forever save me a spot at the next retreat.

Michelle, it is always a joy to receive your wisdom. Thank you for offering encouragement when I needed it most, as an astrologer and a friend. You are a gift.

Brook, there is so much more I could have written about my sessions with you but much of that is sacred, and it all lives in my heart. Thank you for providing such profound healing, especially in my darkest days. I am so grateful to know you.

April, the warmest soul, shining your light on me during our first session when I felt like walking into the ocean. Though we spent only a little time together since we met, the memories you gave me will live in my heart for eternity.

Rashelle, I'll never forget the text you sent me when you read an early draft: "Such a beautiful love story. Between you and DeAndre. Between you and your babies. Between you and yourself." Thank you. I'm beyond lucky to call you my friend.

Tiffany, you helped me turn the "good bones" of my first draft into a new life form, a story with a beating heart and fluttering wings. These words could not have come together in this way without your guidance. These pages you have inspired will be something I cherish with pride forever. Thank you.

Rosie and The Local Salon ladies, thank you all for the fond memories during a time when I needed them most.

To the rest of my top tier Patreon subscribers who allowed me to share sneak peeks of the sometimes messy process: Megan, VeeVee and Earl, Jennifer H.

My early readers, your insight was invaluable in bringing this piece of art together: Vienna, Jillian, Rebecca, Jayne, Annie, Rashelle, Gretchen. Thank you.

My dear friends who held me, emotionally and physically, right after the earth-shattering devastation of my first miscarriage: La'Nette and Megan. I am so happy to call you my friends all these years later.

Megan, our bond is something truly special, and your support has been everything to me. ILYSM.

Mrs. Katchen, the best art teacher I'll ever know. Thank you for nurturing my talent and confidence all throughout high school.

Thank you Megan C., my therapist in New York for many years. You helped me through my first miscarriage when I felt like my world was crumbling. I hope this will reach you.

Ashlee, thank you for providing a warm and caring environment for me through the worst days of my life. You taught me so much during my time on the mat with you and you made me feel like a true badass!

Purdie family, Haley family, the Banks squad! I love you all! You have embraced me as family since day one and I'm so full of gratitude to have you in my life.

Kayla, who helped me polish the final piece while I was stumbling through the process, figuring out how to make this all come together. I'm so glad our paths crossed. Thank you!

To the medical teams—doctors, nurses, and surgeons —who cared for me and cared for us through every tumultuous step, you have my eternal gratitude.

To every woman I met in Mount Shasta, you know who you are. I love you, sisters.

Finally, my late grandmother, Marion, who I know in my heart is watching over my soul babies. And to my soul babies, who are always just a daydream away. This book was a collaboration, the ultimate co-creation—a gift both for you and from you. I love you.

about the author

Mary Purdie is an illustrator living in Los Angeles with her loving husband, DeAndre. Her earliest works of writing and illustration include "The Lost Puppy" (1990) and "The Trouble with School" (1991), both unpublished and written haphazardly with a dull pencil (hey, she was eight-years-old, what did you expect?) Mary finds joy in creating illustrations and pieces of writing that evoke heartfelt emotions. "If You Really Knew Me: A Memoir of Miscarriage and Motherhood" is her first published memoir, but hopefully not her last. Her illustration portfolio can be found on her website: drawnbymary.com

Made in the USA
Las Vegas, NV
04 June 2021

24125214R10142